"As part of my area of expertise in comm̶ ̶ ̶ ̶ ̶ ̶
an open secret that there are three essential qual̶ ̶ ̶ ̶
potential success of a business: proximity, proxin̶ ̶ ̶
becomes clear that despite all the other qualities ̶ ̶ ̶
have, if proximity is not a target, it will fail in its attempt.

Allow me here to make a parallel with the field of financial services in which Marc Bérubé became, in more than one way, a leader. I would say that the three essential qualities are: trust, trust, and trust. Without this aspect, I am convinced that no other quality, even multiplied by a thousand, could supplant the importance of trust.

This confidence Marc was able to show me from our first contact, and to supplement it all, he was able to prove time and time again in his actions, both in my personal file and in the expansion of his cabinet. Indeed, since he started working with me at the beginning of his career, I had firsthand knowledge of his success and evolution. In this field where there are a lot of people called but really few chosen, I can assure that Marc is one of the chosen.

As with any success, we must not just get on top—but we must stay there. Again, I am confident that Marc will stay at the top because he always finds ways to improve with new financial strategies to answer his customer's needs. Moreover, he is not afraid to surround himself with specialists to support him in his business. Because of this, Marc is able to provide a wide range of consulting services and expert partners to support all the financial needs of his customers, even those with very specific needs.

In conclusion, everything comes down to one word—trust—and it embraces many implications! I bet that Marc will continue to meet the challenge of trust with brilliance for many years to come!"

—*Dominic Fournier*, pharmacist and drugstores owner

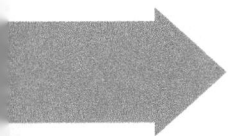

GOING

THE

DISTANCE

GOING THE DISTANCE

LOW-RISK STRATEGIES FOR PROTECTING AND GROWING YOUR WEALTH

MARC BÉRUBÉ

Advantage®

Published by Advantage, Charleston, South Carolina.
Member of Advantage Media Group.

ADVANTAGE is a registered trademark, and the Advantage colophon is a trademark of Advantage Media Group, Inc.

Printed in the United States of America.

ISBN: 978-1-59932-712-9
LCCN: 2016959625

Cover design by Katie Biondo.

This publication is designed to provide accurate and authoritative information in regard to the subject matter covered. It is sold with the understanding that the publisher is not engaged in rendering legal, accounting, or other professional services. If legal advice or other expert assistance is required, the services of a competent professional person should be sought.

Disclaimer: The ideas and strategies presented in this book are for information purposes only and do not constitute actual financial advice. The strategies presented herein are based on the laws governing the insurance industry in Canada at the time of this writing. Those laws are subject to change. Please contact your financial security advisor for specific information on how to implement any of the ideas or strategies presented.

Advantage Media Group is proud to be a part of the Tree Neutral® program. Tree Neutral offsets the number of trees consumed in the production and printing of this book by taking proactive steps such as planting trees in direct proportion to the number of trees used to print books. To learn more about Tree Neutral, please visit **www.treeneutral.com.**

Advantage Media Group is a publisher of business, self-improvement, and professional development books. We help entrepreneurs, business leaders, and professionals share their Stories, Passion, and Knowledge to help others Learn & Grow. Do you have a manuscript or book idea that you would like us to consider for publishing? Please visit **advantagefamily.com** or call **1.866.775.1696.**

To my family, who have supported me through good times and bad.

CONTENTS

GOING THE DISTANCE

SECTION ONE
FINANCIAL-PLANNING STRATEGIES
FOR YOUNG PROFESSIONALS

GETTING IN THE RACE

TRAINING FOR THE MARATHON

SECTION TWO
FINANCIAL-PLANNING STRATEGIES FOR
SUCCESSFUL BUSINESS OWNERS

ADVANCING TO THE PROS

GETTING INTO POSITION
The Importance of Financial Assessment

ACHIEVING ACCELERATION
Strategies for Tax-Efficient Investments

FOREWORD

My responsibilities as a business development director in 1999 allowed me to make a landmark encounter and discover a charismatic young man, enthusiastic and full of energy.

His background as an athlete already demonstrated his determination, discipline, and ambition.

His ability to make contact and maintatin relationships with people with such authenticity was remarkable.

His mining engineering training prepared him to try to avoid and solve problems that may arise, while developing a plan to minimize risk in the short, medium, and long term in the operation of a mine.

This is exactly what he is doing now in the financial security planning field.

His passion to help people toward a better financial life has led to remarkable success during the first years of his career.

In 2002, his career path led him to open Coaching Financier Trek, a financial services firm. This was an avant-garde gesture at the time that allowed him to implement his vision and innovative approaches to problem solving and protection of wealth and heritage for his customers.

Knowing full well himself that sprints are won in seconds, Marc also knows it is very different to prepare for the inevitable things in life. This is often a long journey—similar to a trek.

This philosophy of guidance throughout the financial lives of clients led him to redefine himself and seek partners sharing the same values and goals over the following years.

Several associates have joined Marc's team since then, including Mr. Nicolas St-Vincent, a tax lawyer with expertise in taxation of insurance products, arriving in 2013.

In reading this book, you will learn about innovative strategies and nontraditional problem resolutions. At Coaching Financier Trek, the ultimate goal is to optimize all financial strategies. Marc and his team do this by recognizing the insurance products that often go unrecognized and by establishing a financial process that fosters peace of mind for all customers.

I witness every day the will of Marc and his team to popularize the various strategies described in this book and their passion to help clients achieve financial success.

May the reading of this book motivate you to take the time to pause, to reflect, to listen, to ask for help, and to surround yourself with the right team on the road to your financial wellness.

Hopefully, reading this book will be an inspiration to encourage you to develop strategies, allowing you to achieve your dreams and goals most effectively and with confidence.

Enjoy the reading.

—*Réal Veilleux*

ABOUT THE AUTHOR

Marc Bérubé is the president of Coaching Financier Trek, a Montreal-based financial- advisory firm. The company employs unique strategies using various insurance and annuity products to protect and grow wealth for its clients.

Bérubé began his career as a financial security advisor with London Life in 1999 before founding Coaching Financier Trek in 2002. Today, his twenty-five-member team specializes in helping self-employed professionals and business owners prepare financially to live their dreams.

Bérubé's interesting perspective as a financial security advisor makes him a popular guest speaker throughout Québec. He is often called upon to share his passion and vision for success with professional groups and students at universities across the province of Québec.

Bérubé is a lifetime member of the prestigious Million Dollar Round Table, a global, independent association of more than forty-two thousand of the world's leading life-insurance and financial-services professionals from more than 470 companies in 71 countries. MDRT members must demonstrate exceptional professional knowledge, strict ethical conduct, and outstanding client service. Bérubé is also a member of the MDRT's Court of the Table and currently serves on the organization's Membership Communication Committee (MCC) representing Québec. In 2015, Bérubé was honored to be a guest speaker at the MDRT's annual meeting, held in New Orleans, Louisiana.

Bérubé has also addressed the Young Advisor's Presidents Club of Freedom 55 Financial on several occasions.

A native of Val-d'Or in Québec, Bérubé holds a bachelor of engineering from École Polytechnique de Montreal. He left his mark on the Canadian and international track-and-field scene by setting a Canadian record in the 4 x 200 meter and a Québec record in the 4 x 400 meter during his youth. At the age of eighteen, he ranked among the eight best junior sprinters in the country.

Bérubé's passion for track and field has inspired him to continue running throughout his adult life. In recent years, he has trained for and participated in two ultramarathons, which are footraces longer than the traditional marathon length of 42.195 kilometers. He participated in a Leona Divide 50/50 trail race and later participated in a 70k ultramarathon in western Canada as a funding raiser for a colleague diagnosed with ALS.

Bérubé is involved in the Foundation of Stars and the Heart and Stroke Foundation of Québec, causes that remain close to his heart.

To find out more about Bérubé's unique approach to protecting and growing wealth or to engage him as a keynote speaker at your next event, please contact him using the information below.

COACHING FINANCIER TREK

4020 Louis-B. Mayer, Bureau 308,

Laval, QC H7P 0J1, Canada

514-334-8701 (phone)

877-334-8701 (toll-free)

coachingtrek.com

info@coachingtrek.com

GOING THE DISTANCE

The first time I stepped onto the track at Brigham Young University in Provo, Utah, was one of the most thrilling moments of my life. Richard Crevier, one of Canada's most respected sprint and hurdle specialists, had drafted me to compete in the Canadian track and field trials beind held there. Through his many decades of coaching men's and women's athletic teams, Crevier earned an international reputation in track and field by participating as a coach in numerous competitions including the World Athletics Championships, Olympic Games, World University Games, and Francophone Games. For a seventeen-year-old like me, being in the presence of this preeminent coach was a life-changing experience.

I didn't qualify during those trials, but just being part of such an amazing event further fueled my desire to become a world-class sprinter. When I returned to Québec, I enrolled at the University of Sherbrooke located outside Montreal and continued training with Coach Crevier while working towards a bachelor's degree in physical education. As a sprinter, I always had my eye on the next race, the next win, and setting the next record. My focus paid off . . . for a while.

As a junior athlete, my team and I competed in a number of provincial, national, and international competitions. Competing in the Canadian Junior Championships, I finished eighth in the 100 meter, and my team set a Canadian record in the 4 x 200 meter, breaking an eighteen-year record. (As of this writing, my team's provincial record in the 4 x 200 remains unbroken at the provincial level.) We also set a Québec record in the 4 x 400 meter that has since been broken. In 2011, after seeing a Ray Zehab presentation in Calgary, I decided to begin ultra trail-running training. In 2012, I did a 50k trail run in California and a 70k trail run, which I did to raise $25,000 for the ALS foundation in honor of a colleague who was diagnosed with this disease.

The end to my glory days as a junior athlete came all too soon. Plagued by reoccurring injuries, I was relegated to the sidelines of the sport I loved. When the academic year ended, I returned to my hometown to rethink my career goals and my life. I was eager to get back in the game and to be part of a winning team again, but I did not have a plan to accomplish that.

I grew up in Val-d'Or, a small city located in the Abitibi-Témiscamingue region in southwestern Québec near the La Vérendrye wildlife reserve. French for "Valley of Gold," Val-d'Or is a mining town—gold, zinc, lead, copper—that is also known by tourists for its vast parks and lush forests. I'd spend another year in my hometown, working in a gym, recovering from my injuries, and conferring with family and friends as I struggled to chart a new course for my life. As I rethought my future, I soon realized that teaching physical education was no longer what I wanted to do. I finally decided to earn a degree in mining engineering, a career I believed would keep me in my home of Val-d'Or, where I intended to spend the rest of my life.

I earned my bachelor of engineering from École Polytechnique de Montreal in 1998. When it came time to return to Val-d'Or, mining was in a slump. The price of gold had fallen to about $275 per ounce (today it's $1,200–$1,300 per ounce), and the mines weren't hiring. Once again, my plans for the future swerved off track. As I contemplated my next move, I came to grips with another truth: I'd fallen in love with life in the big city and didn't want to leave. Montreal had a hold on me and had no intention of letting go anytime soon.

Before the ink was dry on my engineering degree, I once again reviewed my career options. Sylvain Rioux, a good friend from my youth in Val-d'Or, suggested I consider working with him at London Life Insurance Company in Montreal. Rioux, who'd earned his degree in business administration, had worked for London Life for about a year and insisted that it was a career that suited me. Of course, I said no a hundred times. "I'm an engineer," I insisted, "and I don't want to be a financial advisor and sell insurance!"

As 1998 drew to a close with no employment prospects on the horizon, Sylvain finally convinced me to meet with the manager of his London Life office. Réal Veilleux explained to me that his office specialized in advising professionals and business owners on how the insurance company's financial products could provide tax advantages and leverage options, as well as be used to protect and, in some cases, grow the wealth of their clients. I was intrigued by the financial strategies Réal and his team used to help ensure the financial futures of their clients.

To earn a degree in engineering, I had to be good with numbers and a problem solver. Conceptualizing a mine, for example, requires an engineer to foresee problems that might happen tomorrow, as well as problems that may occur five, ten, or even thirty years down the road. Taking the long view allows an engineer to develop a plan to minimize or avoid entirely any negative results of a worst-case scenario. Putting together a financial strategy for a professional or business owner requires that same type of thinking. I walked away from my initial conversation with Réal understanding that his company was not in the business of selling one-size-fits-all life-insurance policies to clients. Nor was the company interested in selling products that their clients really didn't need just to make a commission. Réal and Sylvain were in the problem-solving business, which is exactly what I learned to do in engineering school. By the end of my first meeting with Réal, my eyes had started to open to the fact that for him, "selling insurance" had evolved into a passion for helping people live better lives. I decided to stick around for a while to see if I could help them spread the good news.

Three years . . . that's how long I gave myself to make it at London Life. In three years, I believed I'd know if I was any good at the business of financial advising—and it didn't hurt that it would probably take about that amount of time for the mining industry to rebound in case I wasn't.

I decided that if I was going to take a shot at being successful at London Life, it was going to be my best shot. But how did I define success? That question compelled me to devise a clear picture of myself in three years. How much money would I be making? How many vacation days would I be taking? How many clients would I serve? What kind of lifestyle did I want? As I answered these questions for myself, I wrote all my goals on paper and devised a rigorous plan to achieve them. During those three years, I worked hard learning about the industry, the intricacies of the various financial products offered by the company, and all the strategies Réal and his team used to improve the financial lives of their clients. I also enjoyed life in the city when I could. I did something else that I believe made all the difference in my ultimate decision to continue my career in the financial industry: I personally implemented a number of the strategies I'd learned into my own life and purchased a number of the insurance policies I was recommending to others. I did that because I don't think you should be selling a product you don't believe in yourself. I continue to reap the benefits of those decisions today.

In 2002, I left London Life to form Coaching Financier Trek. My friend Sylvain, who had encouraged me along my new career path, came along as a financial security advisor in my new company and remains an important member of our team today. Over the years, my team has grown to twenty-five, including my mentor, Réal, who came on board after he retired from management at London Life. About three years ago, I partnered with Nicolas St-Vincent, a lawyer and tax specialist who is also a financial planner, adding another exciting dimension to my company.

Today, Coaching Financier Trek focuses primarily on providing financial advice and services to two distinct populations: professionals and business owners. Whatever your destination, we'll recommend a route that best meets your aspiration and then help you get there. All our services have one goal: your interests. You can count on our integrity and expertise to develop customized strategies and tips to help you maximize your personal or organizational financial security.

Through Coaching Financier Trek, I've continued my relationship with London Life, primarily through its Freedom 55 Financial division. We also work with other insurance companies and brokerages that allow us to offer our clients many of the financial products available in Canada. This gives us the freedom to recommend what's best for each individual client.

It's been our experience that self-employed professionals often begin their careers with little to no understanding of how to manage their finances or how to plan for their financial futures. We can help them with that—get them on the right path early on so they can focus on their careers.

My special area of focus is helping business owners. Working together, Nicolas and I have developed a nontraditional approach to problem solving as well as to wealth protection and growth that builds on the financial strategies successful business owners might already have in place. We have in-depth knowledge of specific financial products that can reap the greatest tax advantages for business owners. It is at this level that many of our more innovative strategies come into play to the advantage of our clients. There are not many financial security advisors out there who understand these strategies or how to implement them.

True, Coaching Financier Trek isn't like other institutions that can lower the interest rate on your lines of credit by half a percent when you allow them to handle both your investments and insurance needs. But we can offer you an alternative. We provide personal and caring one-on-one service that always has the best interests of you, your family, and your business in mind. I am confident that our innovative approach to life insurance can protect and grow your wealth, as well as save you thousands of dollars in taxes. Using our customized strategies, we do that for our clients every day, and we can do it for you.

The team at Coaching Financier Trek has a passion for working with professionals and successful business owners who share our values. Those who are committed to providing for their families through good times and bad, who care about their employees and the continuation of their businesses, and who give back to their communities are the people our skilled and compassionate financial security advisors are most delighted to help.

Being part of a winning track-and-field team in my youth helped prepare me for my journey as a financial securities advisor. Finding my way back from the injuries that sidelined me during my youth and rediscovering my passion for running in ultramarathons reminds me that our lives—including our financial lives—are all about going the distance. Over the last decade and a half, it has been my privilege to team up with hundreds of professionals and business owners to work together to help ensure the brightest futures for many Canadians.

Sprints are won in seconds, but preparing for the inevitabilities of life is a trek. The path to your more financially successful future begins here.

SECTION ONE

FINANCIAL-PLANNING STRATEGIES FOR YOUNG PROFESSIONALS

CHAPTER 1

GETTING IN THE RACE

REAL-LIFE SCENARIO*

Through the years, it has been my privilege to lead conferences and teach classes about financial-planning strategies on university campuses across the province of Québec. In my experience, the professional education these students receive trains them to become good doctors or dentists or accountants, but all too often they learn very little about how to put together a sound financial plan . . . something they urgently need as they begin making a substantial salary for what is likely the first time in their lives.

A number of years ago, I presided at a conference for pharmacy students on a nearby university campus. My

*Please note: all real-life scenarios, and various details disclosed therein, have been altered to protect client privacy.

audience consisted of ten students who had, through their years of training together, become close friends. As these students graduated and began their careers, eight of them heeded my advice and allowed me to advise them on the first steps to take towards building their wealth over the long term.

While each of these eight students had their own individual needs and circumstances to consider, for those who were married or married with children, I suggested term life insurance. Term life insurance is a simple and inexpensive way to protect a family for a specific number of years in the event of death of the policyholder.

Six or seven years after teaching the class on financial-planning strategies to these ten young, idealistic pharmacists, I received a call from one of them, who informed me of the tragic death of another of these friends in a motorcycle accident. The deceased pharmacist left behind a grieving wife with a newborn baby and a brand new mortgage on their house. Unfortunately, he was one of the two who took my class but never got around to seeing me or any other financial security advisor to ensure the financial stability of his family in just such a circumstance. I realize that a check, no matter how big, can never replace a loved one, but it can provide the means for the family to remain in their home and face the future without the burden of immediate financial worries.

The tragic death of this young pharmacist is never far from my mind. I often think about how circumstances could have been different for his family if he had taken the time to investigate how easy and inexpensive it is to lay a solid foundation for his family's future. I often use the analogy of building a house to illustrate my point. When you decide to build a house, you first think about where you want it, how big you want it, and all the features you want to put into it. But in order for your dream house to survive a lifetime of normal wear and tear, inclement weather, and other natural events, it must be built on a solid foundation designed specifically for that house. And then it must be maintained. The same is true for a financial plan. It's important to build your professional career and your life on a solid foundation, a foundation designed specifically for you and your dreams.

If you are anything like me, the first few years of learning your way around a new career can be an all-consuming process. That said, early in your professional career is the perfect time to begin building your wealth. During our youth, we all expect to make it to retirement in good health and with a bulging financial portfolio. But without putting together a solid financial plan and then pausing from time to time to rethink and adjust that plan to your changing circumstances, all the goals you hoped to achieve in your twenties will not likely play out in your seventies. Even if you do reach retirement age in good health, chances are you will not be in a position to retire and enjoy the fruits of your labors if you don't have a plan in place.

Self-employed professionals—doctors, lawyers, dentists, accountants, engineers, pharmacists, veterinarians—often begin their careers with little to no understanding of how to manage their finances or how to plan for their financial futures. We can help you with that; we can get you on the right path early on so that you can focus on your career.

If you walked into my office today, the first thing I would encourage you to do is dream. Dream big, in fact. Through my years of working with young professionals, I've devised a series of questions I ask to help these professionals really get a vision on what they truly want out of life. Where do you want your career to take you? How much money do you want to earn? How much vacation would you like to take each year? Do you want to own a home? Do you hope to get married? Have children? Drive a Jaguar? Own a cottage on the lake? Build your own business? Support your favorite charities? And so on.

I'm still amazed at how many blank stares I get when I ask these questions. Only when you fully define what is important to you and your future can I help you get to where you want to go. But once you know, that's when the fun begins.

Before I describe the four most important steps that I advise every self-employed professional to take to get in the race to a secure financial future, I'd like to mention an important option available to many professionals in Canada: business incorporation.

I think most professionals are aware of this option, but many don't see the advantages of incorporation. This brief explanation might help.

Beginning in 2001, the profession code in Canada changed to allow professionals to incorporate. Specifically, incorporation is possible only for those professionals governed by a professional body or association. While the laws vary between provinces and between those professional bodies and associations, they typically include dentists, lawyers, physicians, accountants, architects, engineers, and veterinarians. (Check the list in your province to see if it includes your profession.) Incorporating is a personal decision based on your individual circumstances. I encourage you to talk to your lawyer, accountant, financial security advisor, or other trusted professional to determine if and when incorporation is the right move for you.

While there are a few downsides to business incorporation, the income-tax advantages can open up new avenues to help you build your wealth over the long term. Those income-tax advantages include: income-tax deferral, potential-income splitting, and benefit from $800,000 capital gain deduction.

From a financial-planning perspective, I believe the best of these advantages is your ability to defer a substantial portion of the taxes on the income retained by your corporation. In other words, by leaving a portion of your earnings in your corporation, you can defer paying tax on that amount to a time when you are in a lower tax bracket.

Because the tax rates for small businesses are lower than those for an individual, the difference can result in a significant deferral of tax until the income is distributed to the shareholder. The total annual tax deferral is calculated on the difference between the rate you are currently paying on your professional income and the rate your corporation will pay. (Please see chart.)

ANNUAL INCOME	50%*	20%**	DIFFERENCE
$100,000	$50,000	$20,000	$30,000
$150,000	$75,000	$30,000	$45,000
$200,000	$100,000	$40,000	$60,000
$250,000	$125,000	$50,000	$75,000
$300,000	$150,000	$60,000	$90,000
$350,000	$175,000	$70,000	$105,000
$400,000	$200,000	$80,000	$120,000

*Approximate tax on your professional income without a business corporation.

**Approximate tax on benefit up to $500,000 with a business corporation.

While this information is simplified for the purpose of this example, it's clear that the amount of tax that can be deferred is interesting.

With incorporation in mind, it's important to realize that strategies for the individual professional can be vastly different than those for a business. Again, it is important to consult with your lawyer, accountant, financial security advisor or other trusted professional in order to understand all the pros and cons of business incorporation before making the decision to move forward on that. But when done properly at the right time in your professional career, incorporation can play a major role in securing your financial future.

For the purposes of our next discussion, I want to focus on the first strategies you need to put into place as an *individual*. Later on, we'll look at how these first basic steps evolve if and when you become a successful business owner.

With your list of goals in hand, it's time to start training for the marathon.

CHAPTER 2

TRAINING FOR THE MARATHON

When working with self-employed professionals, I think of myself as a "generalist." As a generalist, I look at four aspects of financial planning that my experience tells me are important for all individuals to implement to get their financial health in order for the long term. Remember, sprints are won in seconds, but preparing for the inevitabilities of life is a trek.

By the way, a trek is a journey or trip, especially one involving *difficulty* or *hardship*. A strong financial plan is one that improves your life during the good times but also makes the difficulties and hardships that life throws at you a lot easier to endure along the way.

> **SPRINTS ARE WON IN SECONDS, BUT PREPARING FOR THE INEVITABILITIES OF LIFE IS A TREK.**

The four areas that I encourage self-employed professionals to focus on include cash flow, retirement, living benefits, and death benefits.

The last three involve insurance. Sometimes self-employed professionals just don't know how to deal with insurance. They don't understand all the subtleties of the various insurance products that are out there, not to mention the ones that are best for them. Insurance is complicated. You have your profession to focus on, so there is no need to try to figure it all out on your own. I encourage you to find an insurance specialist you trust to help you. Be sure your advisor has experience working with self-employed professionals like you . . . those earning $100,000 or more. Also note that higher incomes demand different strategies, so find an advisor who will become an active part of your financial team over the long haul.

As you begin training to go the distance in life, remember that small sacrifices early in your career can reap great rewards later on in life.

Let's get started.

CASH FLOW

REAL-LIFE SCENARIO

One morning a few years ago, my assistant received an urgent call at my office from a professional female client of mine.

"I need to talk to Marc right away," she demanded.

"No problem," my assistant replied. "May I tell him why you're calling?"

She replied, "I want to have a baby, and I want Marc to help me!"

My assistant and I laughed about my client's request. What she really wanted was for me to help her and her husband put together a plan that would allow them to start a family without the usual financial burdens that often accompany such a life-changing event.

I'd met with this couple a few months before. At that meeting, I told them that I wanted to be the reference on all their important financial decisions and asked them to stay in touch at least once a year to update their file, and more often if something happens that could impact their finances. Starting a family is definitely one of those things.

I reviewed with her the percentage of her current income she could expect to receive during her maternity leave and how long she'd like to stay home with the child before returning to her profession. We also factored in a little extra to cover some of the initial needs of the baby and for unexpected expenses. By the end of our conversation, my client had a good idea of how much money she and her husband needed to save before starting their family. With a little extra money set aside, I knew they could enjoy becoming parents without the initial financial stress that often comes along with it.

I was happy to help.

Whenever I can encourage my self-employed professional clients to think ahead before they spend their money, I believe I have done a major part of my job. Teaching individuals to manage their finances early in their careers helps prevent having their finances control them later on. It's all about laying that foundation I keep talking about.

Financial difficulty is one of the leading causes of stress for people—stress that can deteriorate your health and damage your relationships. Planning for all the various aspects of your financial life isn't always as easy as running a few numbers and developing a savings strategy in preparation for starting a family. But believe me . . . doing the work to put an appropriate plan in place for all your major expenditures is worth it in the long run.

The crucial first step for self-employed professionals to make the most of their early earning years is to establish a budget. It sounds simple, but you'd be surprised how many people struggle through their entire lives without a sound budget in place. That budget should include everything they will be spending their income on every month.

Cash flow is all about your liquidity. It's your short-term money, the funds you keep on hand to pay your bills, and it's the funds you keep "liquid" for upcoming expenditures and special projects.

If you are a professional such as a doctor or dentist, it's important to remember that you are self-employed and responsible for paying your tax debt at the end of the year. If you were paying attention to the chart in the preceding chapter, you'll know that your taxes could easily be between 35–45 percent of your income. I encourage you to put the money aside for your taxes immediately after receiving each paycheck. Doctors and other self-employed professionals are among the most likely to file for bankruptcy in the early years of their careers because they spent everything they earned every month without planning to pay the taxes they owed. Recovering from bankruptcy is a long, difficult process. Don't let it happen to you.

Your budget includes your debt-repayment strategies for car loans, student loans, mortgages, lines of credit, etc. Do you want to buy a house next year? In three years? In five years? Be sure to have a savings plan for the down payment, and put it in your budget. Cash flow is also about cash accumulation, investment strategies, and the creation of an emergency fund. If you already have an existing investment portfolio, I can't emphasize enough the importance of having your financial security advisor evaluate it and suggest ways to implement tax-efficient investment strategies.

When I work with my professional clients, I often provide the voice of reason when it comes to their goals. For example, if you tell me you want to buy a new car next week, get married next month, buy a new house next summer, and take your three-month-long dream vacation *without* pay soon thereafter, I'll tell you that you can't do all that. As your advisor, it's my responsibility to let you know, based on my years of experience, if and when these projects are viable. It's not that you can't plan for and achieve all of these goals; you'll just have to adjust your timeline.

Where do you see yourself next year? In five years? In ten years? Looking beyond your immediate needs and wants is the real challenge of developing your own personal financial plan, but it's also where you will find the greatest rewards.

Ask yourself, "What's most important to me?" When you figure that out, maybe you'll choose to drive your old car another year or two. Maybe you'll put off buying a house until the summer after next. Maybe you'll take a weeklong vacation this year, and properly save for your big dream vacation that you'll take another time. The best way I know to ruin a vacation is by worrying about how you're going to pay the credit-card bills when they come due at the end of the month. There's so much more enjoyment in taking a vacation you can truly afford.

Let's say that you've decided that saving to buy a house tops your list of goals. So you call me and ask, "How much can I afford?" I always answer that question with another question, "What else do you want to do?"

As an example, by putting aside $1,500 per month, you could have the down payment for your house saved in a year. But what if that means you won't be able to eat out, buy new clothes, or purchase a new car? Saving $1,500 per month may mean you can't get your nails done every week, that you'll have to give up your nights out with your friends at the Montreal Canadiens games, or that your family won't get to spend the holidays with your extended family in another town. What are you willing to give up to save that $1,500 per month? Instead of saving $1,500 per month, perhaps it would better suit your lifestyle to save $750 per month and put off buying a house for two years.

Once they have their down payment saved and are ready to buy the house, I urge my clients to be considerate of their lifestyle. Based on your household income, you may qualify to purchase a house that costs $500,000. The bank will simply calculate its standard ratios and give you a mortgage that will require you to pay every cent of your available cash flow in a house payment. No more nice clothes. No more fishing trips with your buddies. No more university classes towards your master's degree. No funding your retirement account for the future. And you can put your plans to start your own business on hold indefinitely. But what if you were to purchase a house that costs $300,000? What difference would it make to your lifestyle now and to your future?

Some people are willing to make the sacrifices in order to purchase the big, expensive house now, expecting their household income to rise in the future. As a financial security advisor, I urge my clients to think long and hard about what is truly important to them and make their financial decisions accordingly. Often, an objective view of the whole picture can help you weigh the pros and cons of your major financial decisions. Don't hesitate to seek out a financial security advisor you can trust for advice.

Taking control of cash flow (which includes implementing a viable budget) is the first step self-employed professionals need to take towards designing the future of their dreams.

REAL-LIFE SCENARIO

Professionals, especially young ones, often come to me wanting to buy a big house. I encourage them to practice before taking on the big mortgage that usually comes with the big house. Recently, a professional couple came into my office asking me if I thought they could afford a $600,000 home. I made the calculations of how much more it was going to cost them per month to own this large home, which was about $4,000 per month. That included the mortgage payment, the additional taxes, the increase in utilities, and a contingency fund for maintenance and repairs. "It's called planning," I told them. Most young, self-employed professionals suffer from financial problems because they fail to plan properly.

"I'm going to play the bank," I told them. "I'm going to open an account for you, and for the next twelve months, you're going to give me the $4,000, which I'll deposit for you into that account. That way, you will be able to see if a big mortgage payment and all that goes into paying for a big house really fits with your lifestyle."

I've used this "test run" with a number of my professional clients. It gives them the opportunity to truly understand if they can adjust to the change in the amount of disposable income they have every month. Do they like it? Were they forced to skip their vacation because they didn't have the cash on hand? Did they have enough money set aside to replace the tires on the car when they were needed? Did they have to give up shopping for nice clothes or having their favorite wine with friends? Did they have to forego their favorite hobby due to lack of funds? Are they still able to set aside something every month towards their retirement? What about saving to start a family?

TAKING ALL THE BANK OFFERS IS NOT GOOD FINANCIAL PLANNING.

Many people don't plan. They decide they want the big house now. Based on their income and the debt they already owe, the bank declares they can afford to pay the huge mortgage payment. But the bank doesn't take into consideration their customers' lifestyles or their plans for the future. My advice: nobody should ever borrow the amount of money the bank is willing to loan. Taking all the bank offers is not good financial planning. In fact, it's just the opposite of good financial planning.

I explain to my clients that if they decide they don't like setting aside that amount of money every month, they can always come back to me and reduce the amount I'm putting aside for them, or stop the test run altogether, at which time I will close their account and return their money. But the bank won't back off . . . they will always have to pay the big mortgage payment, no matter what. They will be trapped.

I encourage my clients to practice, practice, practice. Putting $4,000 a month away for a year is good, but putting it into their "practice" account for two years is even better. That will give them close to an additional $100,000 to put down on their house. More importantly, they'll know that when they finally buy it, the house will complement, rather than lessen, the lifestyle they enjoy and want to maintain.

It's been my experience that some young professionals can easily handle putting aside the money for a large mortgage. After six or seven months, the couple described in the prior scenario decided they wanted me to deposit less than the $4,000 per month it would take to afford the $600,000 home. We recalculated the monthly expenses around a $400,000 home instead and reset the test run. It didn't take long for the couple to understand that a $400,000 home fit their budget and their lifestyle much better.

Very often, my clients decide they don't need a new home at that time. To me, that's much better than getting involved with a big mortgage that will be nothing but a burden for the short term, and possibly for the long term.

RETIREMENT

At this point, you've created a budget. You are managing your cash flow, and you have a viable plan in place for eliminating your debt. Some financial security advisors believe that you should pay off all of your debt before you begin setting aside money for retirement, but in my view, that's not really effective. If you are a young professional and you're making over $150,000 a year, it's time to develop a plan that will accomplish both. Yes, you can reduce your debt and build your retirement account at the same time. Of course, the interest rate on the specific debt will have to be considered in order to make the right decision.

In 1957, Canada introduced the Registered Retirement Savings Plan to help promote savings for retirement for employees and self-employed citizens.[1] RRSPs, which hold savings and investment assets, have various tax advantages compared to investing outside tax-sheltered accounts. Approved assets that can be held in RRSPs include bonds, income trusts, corporate shares, savings accounts, mutual funds, labor-sponsored funds, and guaranteed-investment certificates. Investing in an RRSP can be complicated, so please seek the advice of a knowledgeable financial security advisor about your options and the risks. Financial security advisors are pros at finding the most tax-efficient strategies that best suit your circumstances.

Contributions made to an RRSP are tax-deductible, and taxes are deferred until the money is withdrawn, usually at retirement, when your marginal tax rate will be lower.

---

1 For more information about the history of RRSPs in Canada, please visit www.canada.com and search "RRSP."

For example, let's say that today your marginal tax rate is close to 50 percent. For every $100 you invest in your RRSP up to your contribution limit, you will save $50 in taxes. Additionally, growth of the investments in your RRSP is tax-sheltered and therefore exempt from any capital-gains taxes or income taxes.

In 2009, Canada started the Tax-Free Savings Account program as a way for adults to set aside money tax-free throughout their lifetimes. Contributions to a TFSA are not deductible for income-tax purposes; however, any amount contributed, as well as any income earned in this type of account, is tax-free, even when it is withdrawn. TFSAs can provide a secondary way for you to save for retirement.

Good retirement planning begins with maximizing your tax-sheltered RRSPs and TFSAs. Because you'll be able to save using these options for a long time, a large amount of money will accumulate for use when you're no longer working. Note that for incorporated professionals, TFSA is not a good way to save because you will have to withdraw money from the corporation, pay taxes, and then invest.

Here's a somewhat simplified explanation of what can happen if you opt for a savings strategy without the tax advantages of a RRSP or TFSA.

Let's say you earn $100,000 per year, and you own an investment that doesn't shelter any earnings it makes from taxes. It's now fifteen years later, and you've accumulated $500,000 in this investment and you've earned 10 percent, or $50,000, in interest on that $500,000. Of that $50,000 you owe half, or $25,000, in taxes.

But remember, you're making $100,000 per year. You already owe nearly half, or $50,000 in taxes, and now the government wants another $25,000, half of what you've earned in interest. But since you're making $100,000 per year, it's unlikely that you'll be able to deal with your tax problem with your current year's income. That means you'll have to sell off part of your investment to pay your taxes.

On December 31, the government calculates the amount of tax you owe on the interest you earn on your investment. What if you don't realize you have to come up with that $25,000 until April, when your accountant gives you the bad news? What happens if the markets are down in April? You have no choice. You will still have to sell off part of your investments to pay your additional taxes, even though they've lost value. So now that $25,000 in additional tax just cost you a lot more. While this sounds like a worst-case scenario, I've seen it happen. I've even had people try to tell me this is a good problem to have because they still made money. I disagree. This is a bad situation when you stop a moment to consider that paying substantial additional taxes could have been avoided altogether.

Earlier I explained that as a self-employed professional, it is likely there will come a time when you will want to incorporate. As a business corporation, you'll have the ability to defer a substantial portion of the taxes on the income retained by the corporation, allowing you to defer paying taxes on that amount to a time, such as retirement, when you are in a lower tax bracket.

For professionals making over $150,000, it's feasible for you to invest in certain tax-efficient life-insurance products that can possibly further fund your retirement. I'll discuss this strategy at length later in this chapter.

RETIREMENT STRATEGY FOR FULLY FUNDING YOUR RRSP

Let me explain an interesting retirement strategy that has worked well for a number of my professional clients.

For this example, let's say that you'd like to put $20,000 into your RRSP this year and that your tax bracket is 50 percent. That means you have to put $1,667 into your RRSP every month in order to reach your retirement goal for the year. I know that sometimes it's really tough to come up with that amount every single month. So instead, I encourage my clients to come up with half. That's $10,000 per year, or $834 per month. At the end of the year, you have sixty days into the New Year to add additional funds to your RRSP for the previous year.

Just before the sixty-day deadline for fully funding your previous year's RRSP, you take the additional $10,000 from your line of credit or from your savings that you've earmarked for another project to get you to your $20,000 annual retirement contribution goal. As I explained earlier, you will receive a tax credit on the amount you put into your RRSP each year. In this case, the $20,000 contribution you made to your RRSP (the $10,000 you accumulated with your monthly contributions + the $10,000 you borrowed from your line of credit or other account) will result in a $10,000 tax credit, which you'll receive back from the government after you file your income-tax return. Once you get your refund check, you simply pay off the $10,000 line of credit or return the funds to your special-project account.

That's called "leverage." But it's safe leverage, unlike when you borrow money to put it into a more volatile investment. If you lose that money, you could be in big trouble financially. But in this case, you're just leveraging that $10,000 for up to sixty days, then putting it back where you got it.

LIVING BENEFITS

REAL-LIFE SCENARIO

One of my clients is a young, self-employed dentist who loves to go mountain biking in his spare time. Mountain bikers often use toe-clip pedals in which the feet are clipped onto the pedals.

My client was at the end of his run and moving slowly, probably too slowly. As he came to a stop, he tried to release his foot from the clip but wasn't able to get it out. Consequently, he fell on his side. Trying to protect himself from getting hurt, he tried to break his fall with both hands, which resulted in a broken thumb on one hand and a broken wrist on the other. A dentist who has casts on both arms is, for all practical purposes, out of work.

My client called me as soon as he could after the accident. I was able to reassure him that after sixty days, the disability insurance he had invested in would kick in and pay him his entire monthly salary for the remaining time he needed to recover. He was then able to sit back and relax, knowing that a mountain-biking accident wouldn't result in a major financial setback that could take months or even years to recover from.

In all my years as a financial security advisor, I wish all the stories I have to tell about professionals becoming disabled had the same happy ending as this one. Fortunately, the dentist recovered quickly from his injuries, but the five months he spent out of work reminded him just how important it was to have a private disability insurance policy in place to protect everything he'd worked for.

If you were a doctor, dentist, or other self-employed professional who suffered from a disabling accident that took a year, two years, or even longer to recover from, how would you cope financially? How would your family deal with the financial burden if all or part of your income suddenly stopped?

Many of my clients throw their hands in the air and retort, "That will never happen to me!" Well actually, your chances of experiencing a disability are higher than you think. Take a look at these statistics.

According to Statistics Canada, about 3.8 million people, or 13.7 percent of Canadians aged fifteen and older, reported being limited in their daily activities because of a disability in 2012. Nearly half of those reporting a disability described their disability as severe or very severe.[2]

In Canada, a thirty-year-old is four times more likely to become disabled than he is of dying before age sixty-five.

One-sixth of Canadians will be disabled for three months or more before the age of fifty. There is also a significant risk that a disability lasting longer than ninety days will occur before you turn sixty-five.[3]

---

2 "Disability in Canada: Initial findings from the Canadian Survey on Disability," Statistics Canada, November 30, 2015, http://www.statcan.gc.ca/pub/89-654-x/89-654-x2013002-eng.htm.

3 Julie Cazzin,"Disability insurance: Preparing for the worst," *MoneySense*, January 30, 2012 http://www.moneysense.ca/magazine-archive/disability-insurance-preparing-for-the-worst/.

As you age, the probability of your becoming disabled falls as the probability of your dying rises.

The chart below demonstrates a typical comparison of the probability of professionals and other office workers throughout North America suffering a disability lasting at least ninety days versus dying in any given year.

Probability of a disability lasting at least ninety days versus death between the age shown in the table and age sixty-five.

AGE	% MORE LIKELY TO BECOME DISABLED THAN DIE	
	MALE	FEMALE
25	32%	147%
30	31%	141%
35	32%	135%
40	32%	125%
45	32%	111%
50	33%	94%
55	32%	79%
60	9.3%	10.6%

Source: https://www.disabilityquotes.com/disability-insurance/stats.cfm

YOUR ABILITY TO WORK IS YOUR MOST VALUABLE ASSET.

The most important aspect of a long-term financial plan for self-employed professionals is private disability insurance. Here's why.

The foundation of your lifelong financial success is built on the money you earn from about age twenty-five until you retire. The amount you'll earn over the course of your career is based on your ability to go to work every day. In fact, your ability to work is your most valuable asset. If you become disabled and can't go to work for a long period of time, everything you worked for up until that point can crash if you don't have an appropriate disability policy in place. You will likely lose everything. Your lifestyle—the one you worked so hard to achieve through years of education and on-the-job experience—depends on your income. In a two-income family, the loss of one of those incomes can be a hardship for the entire family. If you become disabled without an appropriate private disability insurance policy in place, struggling through the first few weeks and months trying to pay the household expenses often turns into a fight to save the house.

Doctors, dentists, and many other professionals are self-employed and making $100,000 and over. Being self-employed means you are responsible for looking out for your family and yourself.

Shopping for disability insurance is not at all like shopping for life insurance, which we talk about in depth later in this chapter. Life insurance is black and white: If you're dead, the insurance company will pay. If you're alive, the insurance company won't.

Disability insurance is all about definitions, exceptions, and exclusions. In Canada, there's a lot of competition among insurers for your business. Buyers beware. If one insurance company's policy costs half as much as another company's policy, the higher-priced policy likely pays out twice as much as the bargain-priced one if you become disabled. In other words, you get what you pay for. If you buy cheap disability insurance, you will get cheap results. So read the fine print. Know what all the definitions, exceptions, and exclusions mean because they make all the difference in the caliber of coverage you'll be getting if you become disabled. Better yet, consult with your trusted financial security advisor—that person who knows the size of your mortgage, the number of children you have heading to college, and all about that new business you've been saving to start. It is in your best interest, and the interest of your loved ones, to purchase the best policy you can afford for your circumstances.

Cheap disability-insurance products often give people a false sense of security. Here's an example of what could happen.

The warm summer afternoon you just spent with your family was wonderful . . . until you tripped over the cat and fell off the back deck. As the ambulance pulls out of your driveway, your mind flashes to that disability policy you purchased three years ago.

You're wondering, *Will my disability insurance cover this?*

Life insurance is black and white, and therefore it's easy to understand. You're either alive or dead, and life insurance doesn't pay when you're alive.

Disability insurance is *not* black and white. Your specific coverage is spelled out in your contract, so it's important to pay attention to the details. All insurers in Canada insure according to the same statistics and the same risks. So ask yourself this: In an industry that's so competitive, how can one insurer come up with a product at half the price of another insurer? The only way that can happen is if that company pays half the number of claims. Exactly what your policy excludes is usually not found in bold type on page one of the contract. In fact, what's on the front page can often be misleading. A policy's exclusions are generally found in the small type on page two. For example, less expensive policies will often include exclusions for back injuries and burnout, two of the main reasons Canadians make disability claims. So buying a higher priced disability insurance policy could likely mean the difference between financial survival and financial disaster in the event you are disabled. You get what you pay for, so if you think you got a great deal on your disability insurance, be prepared to be surprised.

If you are a self-employed professional, chances are you'll receive no coverage at all from your place of work. Just about the time your disability coverage is about to kick in and start paying you a portion of your monthly income, your doctor declares that you are recovering from your three broken bones nicely and are healthy enough to go back to work two days a week for the next three months. That's when the real problems begin. Since you're no longer totally disabled, your bargain-priced disability insurance isn't paying you a cent. Suddenly, you find yourself working two days a week earning 40 percent of your income, which is taxed up to 50 percent. After ninety days, your doctor declares you are well enough to work three days a week for the next three months. Now you're still only making 60 percent of your usual income (and paying taxes on it), and your household bills are piling up, your middle child needs braces, and your spouse's SUV breaks down . . . *again.*

"But premium disability insurance costs a lot of money." I hear that a lot. But consider this: Do you really want to take a chance on cheap disability insurance when a premium disability product will insure your whole salary tax-free until you are able to resume your full schedule and earnings capacity—and will continue to pay you your full salary even if you can never return to work?

Financial security advisors with experience working with various policies have firsthand knowledge of all the pros and cons of the policies they sell, so be sure to seek their advice before making a purchase.

When you have a premium disability-insurance policy, you can say no to the disability insurance on your home mortgage. You don't need it.

You can say no to paying that premium on your car loan that protects you and the bank if you are disabled. You don't need it.

You can say no to paying that credit-card insurance. You have the best disability insurance, which pays you your entire income if you're disabled, so you don't need it.

The money you save on mortgage insurance, car loan insurance, and credit-card insurance is often enough to cover the additional cost of your premium private disability insurance. So, if you get a deal on disability insurance that sounds too good to be true, it is too good to be true.

If you are a self-employed professional, you should also purchase critical-illness insurance. The basic critical-illness policies will pay for three diseases: cancer, stroke, and heart disease. Consider these facts:

⇨ One in three Canadians will suffer a life-threatening cancer during their lifetime.

⇨ One in two heart attack victims in Canada are under the age of sixty-five.

⇨ Every year about fifty thousand Canadians will have a stroke, with about 75 percent left with a permanent disability.[4]

4 Heart and Stroke Foundation of Canada, http://www.heartandstroke.on.ca/site/c.pvI3IeNWJwE/b.3581583/k.BE4C/Home.htm.

Statistics also show that four illnesses are responsible for 90 percent of the claims. They include the three listed previously—cancer, stroke, and heart disease—plus multiple sclerosis. For an additional monthly premium, you can receive critical-illness coverage for about twenty-five more illnesses.

Critical-illness insurance works differently than disability coverage. Let's say you purchased $1 million of expanded critical-illness insurance coverage. You have a heart attack. Thirty-one days later, the insurance company pays you a $1 million tax-free lump sum that you can use for whatever you need or want. (Note: If you don't survive thirty days after the heart attack or the onset of another illness, the insurance company is not obligated to pay.)

Once you receive your lump-sum payout, you might opt to pay for home care or cutting-edge treatment. You might decide on an extended stay at a rehabilitation facility, or you might decide to renovate your house to make it easier for you to get around. You might pay off your mortgage or set aside enough to put your daughter through college. In other words, you can use the money you receive from a critical-illness insurance policy any way you want.

Another great benefit to having critical-illness insurance is that the policies we recommend include Best Doctors, which provides access to the best medical minds in the world. Best Doctors is a company that will look at your diagnosis to make sure it's the correct one and then give you the names of the best doctors in the world who can most effectively treat the type of illness that you have. With the appropriate critical-illness coverage, you can use the lump-sum payout you receive thirty-one days after your diagnosis to get the best treatment in the world.

Here's yet another possibility: As a physician working sixty hours per week in a hospital emergency room, you realize that the stress of the job contributed to your heart attack. Four months after your heart attack, your doctor pronounces you healthy enough to return to your work. With the $1 million lump-sum payout from your critical-illness policy in your bank account, you now have the option of stepping back and figuring out a way to practice medicine in a less stressful situation, one that only requires a regular workweek. Now you have the option to do that while maintaining your lifestyle.

LIVING-BENEFITS STRATEGY

Let me explain an interesting strategy using disability insurance and/or critical-illness insurance that has worked well for a number of my professional clients.

For both types of coverage, there are policies available that allow riders that result in premium reimbursements down the road. For disability insurance, there are policies that provide that if you do not suffer from a disability for seven years, you are entitled to have part of the premium you paid reimbursed to you. For critical-illness coverage, you can get full reimbursement of those premiums in as soon as fifteen years if you did not need to use it.

Let's say you're twenty-five years old and you spend $5,000 per year for protection in the event you suffer a critical illness. If you retire at age sixty without suffering any critical illnesses, the insurance company will reimburse you for every dollar you've paid in over that thirty-five years. That's $175,000. At that point, the cost of your critical-illness insurance for thirty-five years amounts to the interest you could have earned on the $175,000 through the years if you'd put it into another investment. That's a very low-cost product considering that you were protected for all of those thirty-five years against a major financial disaster in the event you had become critically ill.

Also note that for certain critical-illness policies, it is possible to include a rider that states that if you don't survive the required thirty days and die without receiving a payout, the company will reimburse your beneficiaries for the amount you paid in premiums. Per the prior example, your beneficiaries would receive $70,000. Check with your financial security advisor to see if your disability-insurance policy contains this rider.

DEATH BENEFITS

REAL-LIFE SCENARIO

One professional couple I worked with several years ago dreamed of traveling to Tanzania to climb Mount Kilimanjaro. They set about saving and planning for their big adventure to conquer one of the world's most iconic peaks. About thirty-five thousand people from around the world attempt to climb Kilimanjaro, Africa's highest mountain, every year.

One year during Christmastime the two set off on their journey. The wife did not return. My thirty-nine-year-old client suffered a brain swelling on top of that mountain and died.

When I received the message on my telephone regarding her death, I recalled when she and I had met for lunch a few months before. She was questioning the reason she and her husband had life insurance and was not sure she was going to keep the policy. I convinced her to think about it a little longer, and we decided we'd talk about it again after Christmas.

I was overwhelmed with a sense of relief the day the life-insurance check was sent out to her husband. I understand that money can never replace someone you love, but I was still comforted by the fact that he could maintain his lifestyle as he dealt with his sadness and grief.

During my career as a financial security advisor, I have witnessed many situations like the one I describe. All the professionals I work with prefer not to get sick and not to die. But planning for the eventuality of your own death in order to take care of your loved ones later on is a satisfying act of love. If a tragedy takes me away from my family today, at least I know I've done everything I can to prevent them from suffering financially in my absence. As I've stated before, I have a passion for helping self-employed professionals who share my values and my commitment to providing for our families, through good times and bad.

In the preceding pages, we've talked about cash flow, retirement, and living benefits that include disability and critical-illness insurance for self-employed professionals. Your financial plan isn't complete without the addition of life insurance.

During the first twenty to twenty-five years of your career, you need to build a life-insurance portfolio in order to provide for your family in the event of early death. Let's say you're a self-employed professional with a young family and a mortgage. You are earning $250,000 per year and doing fine. But what happens if you're not around anymore? Would your family be able to maintain their lifestyle? Would they be able to keep the house and all the things that make their lives comfortable?

While living benefit policies are all about definitions, exceptions, and exclusions, life insurance is easy—it's black and white, as I've said. It's all about deciding the type of product you need and the amount of coverage you want.

There are two main types of life insurance available in Canada: term and permanent. Professionals just starting out should decide between term and permanent life insurance depending on their circumstances.

TERM LIFE INSURANCE

As its name implies, term life insurance covers you for a specific period of time. It helps young, self-employed professionals cover large, short-term protection needs such as mortgages, student loans, car loans, and other debt at an affordable initial cost. A couple with young children and a mortgage might choose term life as a low-cost way of getting the full coverage they need.

For example, if you are a young, self-employed professional making $250,000 with a family and a mortgage, what happens if you die too soon and your family is suddenly without your income? Death taxes, funeral expenses, unpaid car loans, and student loans on top of the mortgage payments could be overwhelming for the surviving spouse. This type of policy can help your family in this time of need. It allows your family to maintain their current lifestyle if you die, and to stay in the house.

Term life insurance is renewable after ten or twenty years without providing proof of health, but the price will increase with your age at renewal and become substantial in later years. What costs you $400 per year when you were thirty years old can cost as much as $25,000 per year when you're eighty. Depending on the terms of your policy, your coverage will cease once you reach seventy-five, eighty, or eighty-five years of age. If you die after that age, your term life-insurance policy provides you with no coverage whatsoever.

When you are fifty to sixty years old, there may come a time when the mortgage is paid, the children are all grown and out on their own, and you don't need your term life insurance any more. You will likely have the option of converting your term life insurance into a permanent life-insurance policy without proof of health. But your ability to convert can expire as early as age sixty-five or seventy. Again, it's important to understand the details of your policy.

Term life insurance may be all you can afford early in your career. But as your income increases you should either convert to or add permanent life to your insurance portfolio. All too often, I've seen insurance advisors use term insurance to cover a client's permanent insurance needs.

For example, at age thirty-five, a man or woman opts for a ten-year $500,000 term policy that costs $30 per month. When that person reaches forty-five, that same policy is going to cost $75 per month. That's an additional $45 per month, or a 67 percent increase. Let's say the policy owner decides that he or she can still live with that. Ten more years pass, and that same person gets a letter from the insurance company stating that the same policy is now going to cost $300 per month for the next ten years. It may be that the person is healthy and going strong at age fifty-five, but $300 a month, or

$36,000 over the next ten years, is a lot of money. Term life insurance is a lot like rent: if you can't pay it anymore, you get out.

Ten more years pass, and the policy may not be renewable at any cost. Of course, if the policyholder had died during the term of the policy, then it would have paid the beneficiary the $500,000. The reward for a long life is that the money spent on term life insurance over those thirty years is gone. And when the term policyholder eventually dies, is the family prepared to cover death taxes, funeral expenses, etc.? Let's hope so.

The bottom line is this: term life insurance should, in most cases, be considered a short-term solution to a person's overall life-insurance needs. Term life insurance should always be replaced with or converted to permanent life insurance as soon as possible.

TERM LIFE INSURANCE SHOULD, IN MOST CASES, BE CONSIDERED A SHORT-TERM SOLUTION TO A PERSON'S OVERALL LIFE-INSURANCE NEEDS.

PERMANENT LIFE INSURANCE

There's no doubt about it—you're going to die at some point. Dying costs money. On average, it costs about $15,000 in funeral expenses to die in Canada. So you should have permanent life insurance in place as soon as you can afford it—the sooner in your life, the better. Needless to say, permanent life insurance becomes harder to get and more costly as you age.

You buy permanent life insurance at a fixed premium. Again, the younger you are when you buy it, the less your monthly premium will be.

Unlike term life insurance, permanent life insurance continues in force until your death, regardless of your age, as long as you pay your premiums. A good rule of thumb to remember is this: generally speaking, the more a permanent life-insurance policy costs, the less expensive it ends up being in the end. Here's why.

Permanent life insurance has two distinct components. The first is the face value, which is the amount that will be paid to your beneficiaries when you die. Then there is the cash value, which is a savings account that's funded by a portion of your premiums. If the permanent life insurance you choose has a cash value, a portion of your premium will be invested by the insurance company, so it's important to understand the investment risks and the long-term historical returns the insurance company earns on the products you are buying. Again, an experienced financial security advisor can help you understand what to expect.

In the next section of this book, Financial-Planning Strategies for Successful Business Owners, I discuss how certain permanent life-insurance strategies can help enhance your retirement plan.

SECTION TWO

FINANCIAL-PLANNING STRATEGIES FOR SUCCESSFUL BUSINESS OWNERS

CHAPTER 3

ADVANCING
TO THE PROS

REAL-LIFE SCENARIO

It took me several months to set a meeting with a particular Montreal businessman. A highly successful business owner, the man was someone I'd admired through the years, not only because of the company he'd built but also because of his philanthropy.

My business partner, Nicolas St-Vincent, and I were excited by the prospect of possibly working with the man. Once we arrived at his office, we spent a large part of our day reviewing the details of his personal and corporate strategic financial plan. At the end of our extensive analytic process, we both agreed that the businessman was doing everything right . . . that he had everything already in place that he needed to protect and grow his company through any eventuality over the course of the next few years. He was a smart man with a good financial advisor—always a winning combination. We shook the man's hand, thanked him for the privilege of meeting with him, and told him if there was anything we could do for him in the future to please call us.

Nicolas and I weren't disappointed that we couldn't help this prominent business owner improve the financial health of his company. On the contrary, we were delighted to meet a member of the 1 percent of business owners in Québec who were doing everything right. Helping other business owners achieve this level of success is the reason we both go to work every day.

When I began my career as a financial security advisor at London Life in 1998, I remember learning, one by one, the various strategies using insurance products that can be implemented into a strategic financial plan to help protect and grow the wealth of business owners. When I saw the strategies that I put into place work exactly as predicted for one business owner, that victory fueled my passion to help the next client experience the same results. My special area of interest and expertise became optimizing a company's business investments while protecting what it has built through the years. It's the area of my profession that I know I can have the greatest positive impact on the financial success of businesses and business owners across Québec.

As I grew my own business, Coaching Financier Trek, from three employees to twenty-five employees over the last decade and a half, I implemented many of the strategies I discovered into my own strategic financial plan. That means that when I recommend a certain insurance product or strategy to a business client, very often I can say, "This is how it works for me."

Determining whether any of the insurance products or financial strategies I've discovered will work for your successful business begins with a process. The first time I sit down with a business owner, I ask, "When was the last time you called a meeting of all of your business advisors to discuss your company's financial plan?"

How else can you get an objective view of your company's financial health if you don't talk regularly to your chief financial officer and your accountants, tax specialists, lawyers, notaries, insurance agents, and investment counselors? And more importantly, how can you be certain your company has achieved its highest level of financial health if the members of your team aren't talking to each other regularly?

If you've never sat down with your entire financial team, you're not alone. After all, you have a business to run. Chances are, you've never even developed a strategic financial plan because it's too complicated. I see it every day. But it doesn't have to be that way.

Most business owners need objective financial advice from an impartial financial advisor to help them do everything from creating a feasible financial plan, to devising and implementing a major overhaul of their financial strategies, to fine-tuning the plan they currently have in place. That's what I do. I make sure that the owner and the company are protected financially and that all their financial strategies are optimized. It's my job to develop innovative strategies that respond to a business owner's specific needs and wants. I can also help a business owner realign their investments after a period of business growth. In all circumstances, my priority is to do what is best for a business owner.

I never try to sell anyone an insurance product he or she doesn't need. Frankly, I don't need to do that. Once a business owner fully understands the tax advantages, wealth accumulation aspects, and peace of mind that comes with insurance products, they sell themselves.

Calling a meeting of all your financial advisors is an arduous task and probably not at the top of your priority list. Fortunately, there's an alternate way.

Through the years, Nicolas and I have developed a method of taking an in-depth look at a business owner's big financial picture and making recommendations for fixing and/or improving the company's, as well as its owner's, financial health. As a financial security advisor, I specialize in putting the right insurance products in the right places (operating company vs. holding company vs. family trust). And I do that without displacing any members of your existing financial team. If fact, I encourage business owners to beware of any advisors who want to destroy everything that is already in place in order to make their own commissions.

You're already a pro when it comes to running a successful business. Are you ready to advance to the pros with your personal and business finances?

CHAPTER 4

GETTING INTO POSITION

THE IMPORTANCE OF FINANCIAL ASSESSMENT

REAL-LIFE SCENARIO

A couple of years ago, my business partner, Nicolas St-Vincent, and I went into a successful company to conduct an assessment. One of the first things we learned in the course of our investigation was that the business was a partnership between two men.

"Is there a partnership agreement?" we inquired.

"Yes," we were told by one of the partners. "It's in a drawer somewhere."

We pressed the issue, insisting that the partnership agreement would likely have a bearing on any recommendations we might make. After extensive searching, the office assistant finally located the document and presented it to us.

Nicolas, a renowned tax specialist in Québec who has earned the reputation for being among the best specializing in financial products, quickly paged through the document. I instinctively knew exactly what he was looking for. Sure enough, he flipped to the last page and showed it to me. The partnership agreement had never been signed.

Unfortunately, we've seen this happen many times. The partners sit down and hammer out the terms of their partnership arrangement. Then they hire (and pay) a lawyer to put the agreed upon terms into a legal contract. Somehow, during the normal course of their daily business, the two never got around to signing, and thus formalizing, their business arrangement. The unexecuted document was just a stack of worthless paper taking up space in their filing cabinet.

Their business was not being built on a solid foundation, and neither of the partners even knew it. But it was an easy problem to fix.

The process of optimizing your financial investments, both personal and corporate, and protecting what you've built through your years of hard work first requires a comprehensive assessment of your business. This assessment not only gives your financial team insight into what's important to you, but it also helps you focus on what's most important to you.

Do you have plans to expand? Do you need to hire more employees? Do you want your business to continue when you retire? If so, who will take over for you? Do you want your family to maintain its current lifestyle if you unexpectedly become ill, disabled, or die? What happens to the company if you get divorced? What if your partner or other key employee becomes disabled and can't work? Would you like to save more in taxes so you can contribute more money to your favorite charities?

Again, a comprehensive assessment is the first step to putting you into position to optimize your corporate investments and protect what you've built—by helping you to be prepared for anything life might throw at you. But don't worry . . . you won't have to have your entire financial team sitting in your conference room all day in order to get it done.

Working together, Nicolas and I designed a unique assessment process that has already worked for hundreds of business owners across Québec. There are no blanket plans, no cookie-cutter products, and no one-size-fits-all strategies. Our financial assessment is a personal process that allows us to determine exactly what is right for you.

Again, when my partner and I arrive in your conference room, it's important to understand that we're not there to replace any members of your financial team. We see ourselves as additional advisors, four fresh eyes that will bring an all-new perspective of your company to the table. Our complete assessment process may span the course of several meetings in order to allow you, the business owner, and your staff to accumulate the various elements we need to see for our evaluation.

Our assessment works from the bottom up. We make sure we understand both the business owner's family and the business structure. We examine all the legal aspects, including any partnership or shareholder agreements. Of course, you want to build your business on a strong foundation, one that will support anything you put on it. But in finance it takes vision to clearly see where you want to go and to be prepared to get there. In the daily chaos of running your business, it's often difficult to see beyond today, let alone ten, twenty, or even thirty years into the future. Through our assessment, if we can really help you get a clear vision for your future, we can help you get there.

Our assessment process may seem arduous and intrusive, but it often reveals situations that need to be fine-tuned. For example, let's say you are an incorporated doctor with a successful specialty practice earning half a million dollars a year. Your family enjoys a big house, a cottage at the lake, and many other benefits of your hard work. But back when you were just starting out, you took out a small disability-insurance policy and never increased it. In your early years, the $2,000-per-month income the policy pays would have been enough, but now you're making over $40,000 a month. Say that you're suddenly disabled and unable to work. How many months can you get by on the $2,000 a month from your disability insurance? Our assessment process brings to light questions you may not have considered for a long time, maybe even years. We will help you reevaluate your needs and put into place solutions that will provide for you and your family in any eventuality.

It's also important for you to know that my partner and I will conduct this assessment and provide you with a written memorandum outlining our specific recommendations at our own cost. Usually about two to four pages long, our memorandum often suggests that you call on another member of your financial team to accomplish each task. For example, if we recommend that you set up a family trust, or a holding company, which of the professionals you have a relationship with can you call on to do the work? If you don't have someone already on board who you trust to do the job, we can often recommend someone who can help you.

The only thing we ask is that *if* you decide to purchase one or more of the insurance products we recommend, that you buy those products from us. The products are the same price everywhere, so it's not more expensive to buy them from us. Not only will we be there to help you implement the financial strategies related to these insurance products, but we'll also touch base with you from time to time to make sure your circumstances haven't changed and/or your financial plans don't require some fine-tuning.

As a financial security advisor, I bring a number of important skills to the table to help you reach your financial goals. During the course of my workweek, I spend a great deal of my time reviewing the details of various insurance policies so that I can keep up with the latest products available. Whenever I explore a product, I use the problem-solving skills I learned when I earned my degree in engineering: "How can I use this product to solve a problem?" I have access to many products from various Canadian insurance providers, so it's always interesting for me to compare prices and benefits among policies.

Because many of the innovative strategies we put into place involve sheltering income from taxes, we only propose those that we fully believe are within the law. My business partner, Nicolas St-Vincent, is a lawyer and tax specialist. He works to stay on top of the tax laws and fully understands the definitions, exceptions, and exclusions that tend to populate the small print of every insurance policy.

Together with our combined knowledge of insurance-investment products and tax law, we have become a dynamic team in finding ways to help business owners increase their wealth by saving money and lowering their annual tax bill on their investments' rate of return.

Our assessment begins with a lengthy questionnaire. Here is a small sample of some of the questions we ask:

⇨ Are you married, and if so, what type of marriage contract do you have?

⇨ Do you have children?

⇨ Are any of your children involved in your company?

⇨ Do you have a personal retirement plan in place?

⇨ Do you have personal disability, critical illness, and life insurance in place?

First, we strive to fully understand the business owner's family. Once we get the personal details we need, we begin looking at the corporate structure of the business. Here are a few of the questions we ask:

⇨ What type of corporate structure do you have in place?

⇨ Do you have a partner or partners? What does the partnership agreement say?

⇨ Do you have shareholders? What does the shareholders' agreement say?

⇨ Do you have a family trust in place?

⇨ Do you have a holding company? If so, what's in it?

Then it's time to look at your vision for the future. We ask questions like these:

⇨ Are you planning to expand your business?

⇨ What's your time frame?

⇨ Will it require renovation of your current space? The acquisition of one or more new locations? Additional employees?

⇨ Do you plan to sell your business in the future? Or is there a plan for someone else, possibly your child, to take over the business sometime in the future?

⇨ Who will run your business if you are disabled, retire, or die?

⇨ When you die, is your business in a strong enough financial position to pay the death tax without crippling or even bankrupting the business?

As I've said before, we are looking at your business from the ground up. Just as it is with your home, it is essential to build a solid foundation for your business, a foundation that will support everything you plan to build on top of it over time. Unfortunately, when it comes to financial matters, it can be difficult to know if your foundation is adequately supporting your business structure, or if it's starting to crumble beneath it—maybe without you even knowing it. What my partner and I try to do during the assessment phase is to make sure your business has the best foundation possible and that it will sustain what you've built or what you are planning to build in the future.

Our questionnaire also helps us determine what type of risk taker you are. If you are someone who likes to take risks, we can help you balance your high-risk investments with some very low-risk investments. We can also help you diversify your investment portfolio. By that I mean that you should be geographically diversified—with investments in Canadian markets, US markets, European markets, Asian markets, etc.—but also diversified among economic sectors and among management companies. That means spreading your business among three or four different investment companies. The easiest way to accomplish that is to have one broker managing your entire investment portfolio.

Once we gather all the facts that we can through our questionnaire, Nicolas and I are ready to assess the business's current financial situation, including its use of a financial security planning process. We also review the business's balance sheet and monthly budget, as well as evaluate your personal tolerance to risk.

It's also important for us to fully understand your goals. That includes identifying projects you have planned for the short, medium, and long term, and any plans for future purchases.

Our expert information analysis includes establishing a balance between accumulating liquidity and protecting income. Then we can go about the process of selecting financial instruments that can help you achieve your goals. That's where it gets exciting!

WHY UNDERSTANDING YOUR MARITAL CONTRACT IS IMPORTANT

In Québec, there are two types of marital contracts. One contract mandates that in the event of a divorce, the couple splits the value of everything equally, excluding the company. The house, the cottage, the car, and the pension plan are all divided between the marital partners. Another type of marital contract includes the company. That means if one of the partners starts a business, or starts a business during the marriage, the value of the company must be split equally with a spouse if the two divorce. For example, let's say that you spent the early years of your marriage working day and night to build a company that eventually provided a wonderful lifestyle for you and your family. Because of your sacrifices, your company is worth $10 million today. After twenty-five years, irreconcilable differences with your spouse have you on the road to divorce. The question is, does your company have $5 million to pay off your ex-spouse? For most companies, selling off half of the corporate assets is a devastating blow from which they can never recover. Divorce can crash a company. That's why it's so important to carefully consider the type of marital contract you choose.

CHAPTER 5

ACHIEVING ACCELERATION

STRATEGIES FOR TAX-EFFICIENT INVESTMENTS

REAL-LIFE SCENARIO

I met a successful business owner recently whose estate was worth $10 million. Over the course of our conversation, I pointed out that when he died, about $2.5 million would go to pay his taxes. "Do you want me to do something about that?" I asked.

The man shrugged. "My family will get $7.5 million. That's good enough. It's a lot more than I had when I started."

That's true, I thought. *But it's not the most efficient way.*

If you're anything like me, you want your children to start out in life better off than you were when you started out. This man had accumulated much more money than he could spend, so at some point he will have to transfer it . . . to pass it along to his children. It's my job to help him transfer his wealth in the most efficient way possible, and maybe even grow it along the way. So I suggested a strategy in which he could purchase about $200,000 in a life-insurance product that would allow him to give the whole $10 million to his children. At the same time, I was able to increase his wealth and help his company save money by lowering its annual tax bill on the investment's rate of return.

Successful business owners are some of the most stressed-out people on the planet. I know about that firsthand. As a business owner myself, I try to stay on top of my game at the office as I cope with a hectic work environment that includes twenty-five employees and numerous clients, all of whom are important to me. I strive to balance my work life with a fulfilling home life in which I share quality time with my family. I also try to save a piece of myself to give back to my community by working with my favorite charities, the Foundation of Stars and the Heart and Stroke Foundation of Québec. And I can't forget the speaking engagements I accept in order to educate young professionals and others about the importance of putting together a solid financial plan early in their careers. Of course I want to spend the occasional weekend fishing with my friends, traveling, or engaging in my other hobbies. Who doesn't, right? And my wife won't let me forget about the ongoing maintenance that needs to be done around the house.

As a successful business owner, you get it. Life can be hectic.

In addition to coping with "normal life," I often meet success-ful business owners who have 90 percent or more of their net worth wrapped up in the assets of their business. That's like having most of your money invested into one company stock. If your holding company has invested in the financial markets, anything could happen. You could wake up one morning to the realization that you've lost a portion of your net worth or even lost everything. Your workweek is further burdened with all the stress caused by your constant need to follow the financial markets. Running a business is difficult enough without having high risk hanging over your head.

But there's a better way, one that can give you the peace of mind you need about the future of your company and the future of your family and will allow you to sleep a little better at night. Why not start putting something aside that will not be so affected by the financial markets? I'm not suggesting that you pull all your money out of the markets, but I do encourage you to choose your investments wisely. Don't just look at your rate of return; look at your rate of return after taxes. Don't listen to your stockbroker bragging about the 8 to 10 percent you made on your portfolio last year without telling you how it's going to be taxed. The money you make from your investments can be taxed from 25 percent to 50 percent. If you made a 10 percent rate of return on an investment that was taxed at 50 percent, then the reality is that you only made a 5 percent rate of return.

Building an insurance portfolio is a safe and cost-effective way to protect your financial success throughout your work life and then be able to retire in the lifestyle you and your family are used to.

When you use a portion of your assets to build an insurance portfolio, there are a number of strategies that can be put into place to protect and grow your wealth that are low risk. These proven strategies will get you a fair return on your investments without you having to beat the market, day in and day out. So when you build an insurance portfolio that allows you to take advantage of these strategies, you'll lower the taxes on your investments. That's where you'll make money. The other bonus to building a strategic insurance portfolio is that both your business and your family will be in a better financial position to deal with any of the various inevitabilities that life throws at you.

There aren't many players in the arena of financial-planning experts these days using this method of protecting and building wealth for their business clients because it's inherently more difficult to develop a plan using these products. It's just not as easy as using more traditional investments, so many financial advisors don't do it. But this is what I do every day. After completing a thorough evaluation of your business, I know which of these strategies will work in your specific circumstances. Once that's determined, it's also important to note that with the insurance products and strategies we implement, we have control of the outcome. We know that what we promise will happen.

ABOUT PARTICIPATING LIFE INSURANCE

The whole life-insurance product I normally recommend to my clients is what is referred to as "participating life insurance." A form of permanent life insurance, this type of policy features a tax-preferred savings component. Participating life insurance also provides an opportunity for policyholders to earn dividends, although they are not guaranteed. The policyholders don't have the burden of "beating the markets" because the insurance companies' skilled team of market experts manage the investment portion of its participating policy products.

When dividends are earned, they can be used to reduce out-of-pocket premiums or to purchase additional life insurance. Participating life-insurance products also include a choice of riders and benefits that can be added to the basic policy. I often use these riders and benefits to develop an innovative strategy to meet a client's specific needs and circumstances.

STRATEGY IN LIEU OF DECLARING A DIVIDEND

As an example, let's say you are a successful business owner who is forty years of age. Your business is doing very well these days, and a lot of money is flowing into your holding company. One of the highly successful investments you made resulted in a 10 percent rate of return, or $100,000. Normally, you will have to pay 50 percent of that, or $50,000, in taxes. So after taxes, you made $50,000 that is now sitting in your holding company.

You'd like to take that money out of your holding company and put it into your own pocket. To do that, you'll have to declare a dividend and pay more taxes. So of the $100,000 you made in the markets, you should manage to hang on to $35,000 or so. Before you declare, "But I still made money!" take a look at this strategy.

Let's say that instead of investing in the volatile financial markets, you put some of your profits into a tax-preferred life-insurance policy. At age sixty-five, it has grown into $1 million. You would love to start enjoying some of that but don't want to declare a dividend because of the huge amount of taxes you'll owe. I can help you arrange to take out a personal line of credit from the bank for 90 percent, or

$900,000, which you will guarantee with the asset of a life-insurance policy. (It goes without saying that the value of the life-insurance policy is well in excess of $1 million in this example.) Now you have access to the $900,000 tax-free. When you die, your life-insurance payout will go into your holding company, a portion of which will be used to repay $900,000, plus interest to the bank. In Canada, when you receive the proceeds from life insurance, no matter the amount, it is available with low tax to the succession of the business owner through the capital dividend account (CDA)

To recap, the business owner has a $900,000 debt that was guaranteed with the money from a life-insurance policy. When the owner dies, there's a larger amount of money—let's say in this case it was a $3 million death benefit, which flows into the company's capital dividend account tax-free. The succession will then pay back the $900,000 in debt, plus interest to cover the owner's line of credit, and then be able to keep the additional $2 million and get it through the CDA. The owner's life insurance has just saved a whole lot of money in taxes. That's a no-brainer. It's what you should do. It just takes planning and foresight to reap this level of return on your corporate investments. Note: this is a leverage strategy and should be looked at very carefully by your professionals.

STRATEGIES FOR INDIVIDUALS WITH LARGE REAL ESTATE HOLDINGS

My company often works with successful business owners who have invested in a large amount of real estate. Their asset is huge, maybe even one hundred to two hundred doors, but they don't have much cash flow because their money is all in bricks.

As an example, let's say you're a sixty-five-year-old real estate investor with $50 million worth of real estate that you purchased through the years for only $40 million. When you die, your company will owe taxes on the increased value of your properties of about 25 percent. That's a tax liability of $2.5 million.

The owner of the real estate often believes that his or her beneficiaries can take a mortgage on some of the real estate in order to pay the $2.5 million owed in taxes. While that is possible, I often see that the owner has already taken out a loan on the equity of one or more properties in order to buy another property.

But let's say it is possible to get a loan on the equity of one or more properties. It's important to note here that while the interest the owner pays on loans to finance the purchase of another property is tax-deductible, if you borrow money against the equity of your properties to pay the taxes, the interest rate becomes nondeductible. That makes this option less attractive.

Therefore, you need a life-insurance policy worth $2.5 million that will pay out upon your death to cover your taxes. Based on your age (sixty-five) and other factors, that life insurance will cost you $125,000 per year.

No way! If you're anything like most real estate investors, you don't have that kind of money lying around every year to pay for life insurance. Through the years, whenever you got a windfall, you reinvested it into more real estate. That's how you managed to build your company's real estate holdings to $50 million.

But what if you could get the insurance paid for you every year without taking one cent out of your pocket? Would you do it then?

I have an innovative strategy for that, and here's how it works: We work with the bank to pay the premium on your life-insurance policy every year through a line of credit it opens for the business. The business will pay the annual life-insurance premium from this line of credit. Initially, that line of credit will be guaranteed by the cash value of the life insurance and the real estate properties. After approximately fifteen years, the type of life-insurance policy we normally use will have enough cash value to cover the line of credit. At that point, using the real estate to guarantee the line of credit will no longer be necessary.

We work to make sure that there is enough life insurance in place to repay the line of credit, as well as all the taxes that will be owed upon your death. All of this will not affect cash flow. All it took was for us to leverage a small amount of the real estate that you already owned. The succession will keep the real estate you built.

This is another interesting strategy. You need the life-insurance coverage because you don't want your succession to have to sell a large percentage of your assets to pay the taxes that will be owed when you die. With this innovative strategy, you get all the insurance you need, and it doesn't affect your cash flow. So what do you do? The answer is simple: you do it.

CHAPTER 6

COPING WITH GAME CHANGERS

STRATEGIES FOR BUSINESS CONTINUITY IN THE EVENT OF DISABILITY, CRITICAL ILLNESS, OR DEATH

REAL-LIFE SCENARIO

Late last year, I was giving a presentation to a partnership. As I was explaining the importance of having the company carry life and disability insurance on the partners in order to protect the company, one of the partners interrupted me. He told me he had a close friend who owned a successful business with a partner but did not have a partnership agreement. One day, his friend's partner was injured in a serious motorcycle accident and suffered a severe head injury that left him in a vegetative state. Because the injured man's mother is his legal guardian with power of attorney, she is now the acting partner in the company, making decisions about a business she knows nothing about. The remaining partner is now working twice as hard and answering to his partner's mother. If the mother decides to sell the shares of her son's business at some point, she can sell them to anyone, even to the biggest competitor of the company.

This all could have been avoided with a partnership agreement funded by disability-insurance products for the partners.

As a business owner, have you ever considered what will happen to your business in the event of a disability, critical illness, or the death of yourself or another key employee? Could such a circumstance harm or even destroy the company you've worked so hard to build over the years?

THE IMPORTANCE OF DISABILITY AND CRITICAL-ILLNESS INSURANCE

Whether you are a young professional or a successful business owner, it is important to have an appropriate amount of disability and critical-illness insurance in the event something unexpected happens. The income you'll earn over the course of your work life is based on your ability to go to work every day. In fact, your ability to work is your most valuable asset. But if you become disabled and can't go to work for a long period of time, everything you worked for up until that point can crash if you don't have an appropriate amount of disability coverage in place. I'm not exaggerating when I say that you could lose everything, because I've seen it happen all too often. Your lifestyle—the one you worked so hard to achieve through the years—depends on your income. Without an appropriate amount of disability insurance in place, the struggle to pay household expenses during the first weeks and months after a debilitating event often turns into a fight to save the house. This important coverage will pay you a monthly income—depending on the amount of coverage you purchased—for the length of your disability.

If you are a successful business owner, you should also purchase critical-illness insurance. The basic critical-illness policies will pay for three diseases: cancer, stroke, and heart disease. Experience shows that four illnesses are responsible for about 80 percent of the claims.[5] They include the three diseases listed plus multiple sclerosis. For an additional monthly premium, you can receive critical-illness insurance that includes coverage for about twenty-five additional illnesses. Unlike disability insurance, critical illness coverage provides you a tax-free lump-sum payout so that you will have extra cash on hand to cover additional expenses related to your illness. It's important to note that you can use the money you receive from this insurance in any way you want. You become eligible to receive your lump-sum payout from critical-illness insurance thirty-one days after your diagnosis.

Another great benefit to having critical-illness insurance is that the policies we recommend include Best Doctors, which provides access to the best medical minds in the world. Best Doctors is a company that will look at your diagnosis to make sure it's the correct one. Then they will give you the names of the best doctors in the world for treating the type of illness that you have. With your lump-sum payout in hand, you will be able to seek out treatment from those doctors, if you choose.

5 Legal & General, 2015 Claims Report—Critical Illness and Terminal Illness, 2015, http://www.legalandgeneral.com/library/protection/sales-aid/W13943.pdf.

CORPORATE STRATEGY TO PAY FOR CRITICAL-ILLNESS COVERAGE

Here's something amazing you may not know: you can have your corporation purchase your critical-illness and life-insurance coverage. That makes your business the owner of the policy and beneficiary, and you are the insuree, or the person who is insured. Because your corporation owns the policy, the premiums are paid with corporate profits that were only taxed at the corporate rate of about 19 percent, which is better than coming out of your own income, which is taxed up to 53 percent.

Let's say you're forty or forty-five years of age. Your company is growing and doing well. The only thing that can interfere with your healthy business is an accident or a serious illness on your part that requires an extended period of recovery. When something of that nature happens, everything could fall apart. If you have the appropriate insurance in place, the result of your absence does not have to be catastrophic to the business you've worked so hard to build—instead, if you become disabled or critically ill, the insurance carrier pays the benefits directly to your company, which owns the policy. Therefore, your company is financially protected in the event that you're not there to run it. The company is able to use the money to hire others to handle your responsibilities until you are able to resume work. Having this coverage in place just makes good business sense.

What if nothing happens and no benefits are ever drawn on the coverage? After fifteen years paying the annual premiums on the coverage. Here's an example of how it could work: After fifteen years, your company can opt to cancel the disability and/or critical-illness insurance coverage. At that point, everything your company has paid in premiums through the years is reimbursed to the corp, but through a split-dollar agreement, the money can be reimbursed to you, the insuree, tax-free. This is an amazing strategy, one every successful business owner should be using.

THE IMPORTANCE OF DISABILITY-BUYOUT INSURANCE

If you or one of your business partners became disabled and was unable to work for a long period of time or indefinitely, would this unfortunate situation have a major impact on the operation of the business? In most cases, the answer is an emphatic "yes."

A disabled owner or partner often represents a dual liability to the company. First, the company will likely have to continue paying the disabled person's salary during the time he or she is unable to work. Second, the remaining owner(s) or partner(s) will have to take up the slack caused by the absence of the disabled person.

By purchasing a disability-buyout insurance policy before a disability happens, the business can provide a mutually agreeable solution for this difficult situation. This type of policy is specifically designed to pay an amount equal to a prearranged buyout amount agreed to by the owners. Most commonly, the buyout provision is paid in a lump sum; however, a plan can permit the buyout to occur through the use of periodic income payments, if desired.

Disability-buyout insurance policies have an "elimination period" of between twelve and twenty-four months to limit the dual liability often caused by a disabled owner or partner. This elimination period provides enough time to determine whether the disabled person will or will not be able to return to work at the business.

THE IMPORTANCE OF LIFE INSURANCE

REAL-LIFE SCENARIO

Not long ago, I met a young woman who owned a pharmacy. A real go-getter at the young age of thirty-two, this woman was well on her way to a successful career. As I explained the tax advantages of permanent life insurance and its ability to grow cash values, the young woman seemed only moderately interested. She said she needed time to think about what I'd told her.

Two months later, the woman came to see me. She had just returned from a conference of pharmacy owners. At the conference, she'd had the opportunity to talk to a sixty-year-old pharmacy owner about the same type of participating life insurance I had talked to her about a few weeks previous. "I wish I would have taken more," he told her. "If I knew at your age what I know now, I would have taken a lot more insurance."

The young pharmacy owner was convinced. She signed up for life insurance on the spot.

There's no doubt that you are going to die at some point, so you need to have permanent life insurance in place as soon as you can afford it—the sooner the better.

Needless to say, permanent life insurance becomes harder to get and more costly as you age. You buy permanent life insurance at a fixed premium. Again, the younger you are when you begin investing in a high-quality life-insurance policy, the less your monthly premium will be.

Unlike term life insurance, permanent life insurance continues in force until your death, regardless of your age, as long as you pay your premiums. Permanent life insurance has two distinct components. The first is the face value, which is the amount that will be paid to your beneficiaries when you die. Then there is the cash value, which is a money accumulation that's funded by a portion of your premiums. If the permanent life insurance you choose has a cash value, it's important to understand the investment risks and the long-term historical return on the products you are buying. Consult with your financial security advisor to learn all the facts before you invest in any life-insurance coverage.

On average, it costs $15,000 or more in funeral expenses to die in Canada. If you are a successful business owner, you will likely have to pay death taxes on your wealth unless a transfer to your spouse is done. Your beneficiaries won't have to pay taxes on the increase in value of your primary home, but if you own a vacation cottage, a duplex you rent out, or other real estate, taxes will be owed on the increase in the value since you purchased the property or properties. Dying in Canada can be a costly proposition, especially if you haven't sat down with a trusted financial advisor and planned for the inevitable.

The first step is to calculate about how much money you will owe in taxes when you die. The best way to pay your death taxes is through life insurance. Chances are, you've spent years building your business. You have always planned to pass your vacation cottage or other assets on to your children, but without enough life insurance in place, your beneficiaries may be forced to sell off some of your assets, or even your business, in order to pay all the taxes due. So it's important to have enough life insurance to cover all these expenditures. This is a job for permanent life insurance.

I mentioned participating life insurance in the preceding chapter, but it's worth repeating here. Participating life is a form of permanent life insurance I often recommend to my clients, because this type of policy features a tax-preferred savings component with vested cash values. Participating life insurance provides an opportunity for policyholders to earn dividends, although they are not guaranteed. The policyholders don't have the burden of "beating the markets," because the insurance company's skilled team of market experts manage the investment portion of its participating-policy products.

With a good participating policy on the market, you will likely earn a rate of return on the investment portion of your policy. When dividends are earned, they can be used to reduce out-of-pocket premiums or to purchase additional life insurance. Or you can choose to have your "participation" sent to you by check every year, but you will have to pay taxes on that amount.

I always recommend that your annual participation be added to your cash value, which shows up as an asset on your company's balance sheet. I pointed out earlier that permanent life insurance has two distinct components: the face value, which is the amount that will be paid to your beneficiaries when you die, and the cash value, which is a cash accumulation that's funded by a portion of your premiums. There are some insurance products that are very effective at building large cash values, and these are the products you are looking for. There's a maximum amount of money you can legally accumulate into this type of product every year, but you don't have to pay taxes on that accumulated money until you take it out.

With this type of policy, it's fun to look for that breakeven point where the amount you paid in is about equal to your cash value. That usually happens around the eight-to-twelve-year point. For example, you've paid $25,000 a year into your participating life insurance for a period of ten years, or $250,000. At that point in time, the cash value of your policy is also about $250,000, so your life insurance has cost you close to nothing.

Now let's say you continue paying for the policy another ten years, for a total of twenty years. That's $25,000 per year for twenty years, or $500,000. But the cash value of your policy is now $675,000 to 750,000! You have much more in cash value than you paid in premiums. After twenty years, it's possible that you don't have to pay the premiums anymore, but the cash value continues to increase. It's even possible to draw out a portion or all of the cash value to use in retirement. But remember, you'll have to pay taxes on any money you receive.

⇨ Not quite ready to pay large annual insurance premiums? If you're still insurable, you might consider buying a term life-insurance policy that you can convert into permanent life insurance when you're ready—without any proof of insurability.

STRATEGY FOR INSURING THE PARENTS OF A BUSINESS OWNER

When a company buys life-insurance coverage, any death benefits paid have a special status. Those death benefits go directly into a capital dividend account. A CDA is a corporate account that gives shareholders designated capital dividends with no or low tax.

Here's a strategy we use for our clients who are about forty-five to fifty-five years old. You can take out life insurance on your parents, provided your parents agree.

You begin by individually taking out the life-insurance policy on your parents. The day the policy is issued, you transfer it to your holding company. You are legally able to transfer this property, making your holding company the beneficiary and the payer of all premiums. In this circumstance, you will never have to pay the premiums personally; it's only the company that will pay the premiums. So the premiums are paid with the company's tax rate, around 20 percent.

Normally your parent will die between twenty-five or thirty years before you, so you will get the death benefit into your holding company through the CDA with no or low tax.

Let's say your parents lived to be very old and the premiums your company paid were equal to the death benefit. There's still a tax advantage to purchasing the life insurance coverage this way. The difference is, now you can take the money out of your company's account tax-free. If you had taken the amount of the premium your company was paying every month and put it into your pocket instead, you would have had to pay the 40 percent tax on the dividend.

It is important that your siblings understand this strategy before you put it into place. They need to know that since your company is paying the premiums, the company will receive the death benefit, not them. Nothing is worth creating a family rift that could last for years.

BACK-TO-BACK STRATEGY FOR PROTECTING YOUR WEALTH

Let's say your business has been very successful through the years, so at age sixty-five you decide to sell your company and retire. The business is now someone else's responsibility, but you still have $20 million in your holding company. Let's say that over the next ten to twenty years, you really enjoy life and spend $10 million out of your holding company. Therefore, your holding company, worth zero dollars at the beginning, is now worth $10 million. That means there's a capital gain of $10 million in your company—the increase of value from zero to $10 million. In Canada, your beneficiaries will have to pay 25 percent tax on the capital gains, which is based on your final tax return. That's $2.5 million going straight to the tax when you die. Now your beneficiaries have a holding company worth $7.5 million in bank accounts and other investments. If they want to put any of that $7.5 million into their own pockets, they will have to declare a dividend and pay an additional 40 percent, more or less, on the $7.5 million that's left.

Now the $10 million holding company you left to your loved ones is worth $4.5 million. (That's $10 million – $2.5 million in capital-gains tax – $3 million in tax on dividends.)

If you'd like more of the money you've worked hard to earn over the years go to your beneficiaries upon your death, there's an interesting way to accomplish that. In fact, your heirs can avoid the 40 percent tax on dividends with an appropriate plan in place prior to your death.

Let's adjust the outcome of the scenario. You are now seventy years old. Instead of leaving the $10 million in the holding company to share with the taxes upon your death, your corporation decides to invest in an annuity. While a life-insurance policy is based on the premise that you give them small amounts of money over time and then the insurance company will give you (as in your beneficiaries) a large amount later, an annuity is the opposite. With an annuity, you give the insurance company a large amount of money, and they will give you small amounts of money over time. For the $10 million, let's say the insurance company has agreed to pay you $500,000 per year in an annuity payment for the rest of your life. But before you write that check out of your holding company, there's another step you need to take.

Now you need to purchase a life-insurance policy with a face value of $10 million. You will have to purchase this life insurance from a company other than the one from which you bought the annuity. Because you are now seventy years old, the life insurance premium will be costly, say upwards of $125,000 annually. Of course, the life insurance premium will vary depending on your health. But even if the life-insurance premium is $1 million, the annuity will give you more or less the $1 million because the annuity and the life insurance are based on a similar mortality table.

Now is the time to write that $10 million check out of your holding company made payable to the annuity company, leaving your holding company valued at zero. That means there will be no capital-gains taxes owed upon your death and no 40 percent dividend taxes owed when your loved ones take the money you meant for them.

Every year for the rest of your life, you will take the $125,000 you receive from the annuity company and pay for your life insurance. Then when you finally get around to dying, the life-insurance company will pay $10 million into your CDA, which will allow your beneficiaries to take their inheritance with no or low tax.

This is an amazing strategy. If you are still insurable, this is undoubtedly the best way to protect your wealth, and it's risk-free. There is no investment in the world that compares to this—no investment in the world in which the entire $10 million you won't need will go to your family.

WE DON'T TRY TO BEAT THE MARKETS; INSTEAD, WE BEAT THE TAXES.

We always tell our clients that we don't try to beat the markets. Instead, we beat the taxes. We follow the law, but we use it in our clients' favor. This strategy is clean . . . there's no gray area. We call this the corporate back-to-back strategy. That's an annuity backed by life insurance.

CHAPTER 7

OVERCOMING HURDLES

STRATEGIES FOR THE PROTECTION OF KEY PERSONNEL

REAL-LIFE SCENARIO

We are working on a case right now in which there is one key employee who is also a partner serving as the president and CEO of a company. He's the only partner who has anything to do with the operation of the business. The other two are silent partners who helped finance the business.

If suddenly this one man is disabled, contracts a critical illness, or dies, the company would likely crash. Because he's so important to the continuation of the business, we are working to make sure that the company purchases large insurance policies on him. We're talking about $7 million of life insurance and probably the maximum we can get in critical illness in Canada, which is $2.5 million. If he dies, there will probably be enough in life insurance to reimburse the investors. In the event of a disability or critical illness, there may be enough to hire another CEO to replace him to prevent the business from falling apart.

IN THE EVENT OF DISABILITY

Having a plan in place in the event that a key employee is disabled is often the difference between survival and failure of your company. One of the vital pieces of information we collect during our initial assessment of your business is an overview of your key employee personnel. What vital functions is each person responsible for? How difficult would it be to replace that person if suddenly they weren't there for a month, six months, a year, or ever?

As the business owner, if you're also a key employee, you need to ask yourself what will happen if you're unable to be there over an extended period of time. At what point will the business actually start to fail? If your company is large enough, with a number of vice presidents and a big structure, maybe everything in the business will be as usual in your absence. You will still have your income coming in through the continuation of your salary and dividends.

But most of the companies we work with are medium-sized businesses in which the president/owner is still the top, key person in the company. He or she is the person who handles all the company's contracts and brings all or a large number of the clients to the table. If the owner isn't there to keep the company operating as usual, the business could begin to fail quickly. This is where disability insurance comes into play.

As an owner of a successful medium-sized business, you wouldn't want your business to bear the burden of having to pay your salary as well as the salary for your replacement at the same time. For example, if your salary is $150,000 per year, you need to have disability insurance in place to cover that entire amount so that there are funds available to hire someone to manage the company while you're out on disability.

Business owners can be very tough on themselves. Many of them say that even if they break a leg or are in a wheelchair, they will still be able to get back to work. But having your company purchase disability insurance will cover your salary while you recuperate from an injury that has you disabled for a period of months. In the event of more serious disabilities, it will cover you for years.

The normal disability-insurance product we most often recommend will cover the owner's salary until he's age sixty-five. For example, if he becomes totally disabled at age fifty, he will still draw his full salary until he's sixty-five.

The same principle applies when you have partners in the company. As an example, let's say your company has three partners, all key people with different responsibilities. If one partner becomes disabled, the two remaining partners don't need the financial burden of paying the disabled partner's salary while having to hire someone else to cover his important responsibilities.

Similarly, your company can provide disability insurance for other key employees.

IN THE EVENT OF CRITICAL ILLNESS

Over the usual course of my work life, I meet many business owners in their fifties who seem to have it all. Their business is successful, money is flowing, and everything is on track for a perfect retirement at age sixty. I ask them this question: "Other than something completely out of your control such as a massive-market failure, what's the one thing that could go wrong that could completely derail your plans, to potentially destroy everything you've worked for over the years?" The answer almost always is, "A critical illness."

Many business owners believe that a critical illness will never happen to them. Unfortunately, it happens to good people every day. So it's important to consider what happens to your company if you suffer a stroke or a heart attack or are diagnosed with cancer, Parkinson's disease, multiple sclerosis, or some other devastating disease. And what happens to your family?

It is easy to protect the future of your company in the event you suffer a critical illness along the way. Your company can purchase critical-illness coverage that can pay up to $2.5 million in a lump sum once you survive thirty days after your diagnosis. Here's something else amazing you may not know: you can have your corporation purchase critical-illness insurance on you to protect your company in the event you can't be there.

Let's say you suffer a heart attack—on day thirty-one after your heart attack, the insurance company will send your company a check for the full amount of your coverage. If you have the appropriate insurance in place, the result of your absence does not have to be catastrophic to the business you've worked so hard to build. The insurance carrier pays the benefits directly to your company, which owns the policy. Therefore, your company is financially protected in the event that you're not there to run it. The company is able to use the money to hire others to handle your responsibilities until you are able to resume work, if ever.

Once your company receives the lump-sum payout, you can also take a dividend from your company to help you and your family meet your financial responsibilities through your recovery. It's worth mentioning again that certain critical-illness policies offer Best Doctors coverage. Once you are diagnosed, Best Doctors will review your diagnosis, often going deeper to give you a more precise diagnosis. Then the company will direct you to the best practitioners in the world for your critical illness. If you decide to receive treatment from one of the best, you will have the money available through the critical-illness insurance policy taken out by your company, which you can take through a dividend.

SPLIT-DOLLAR STRATEGY

Consider this: let's say an operating company pays all the premiums for the critical illness coverage for a business owner. After fifteen years, we can have 100 percent of the premiums paid by the company returned to the business owner with low taxes on it.

Here's how it works. Let's say your company pays a premium of $25,000 per year for a critical-illness policy that gives the company $1 million of protection. If you never have to use the insurance, you can receive full reimbursement of the premiums, totaling $375,000, paid directly to you after fifteen years.

There's a tax advantage to doing this. In the normal course of business, if you wanted to take $375,000 out of your operating account to put in your own pocket, you would have to pay close to

40 percent tax on your dividend, or $146,250. In this scenario, you send your premiums to the insurer every year, and in fifteen years you can cancel the critical-illness insurance and get reimbursed for all or part of the total amount of premiums your company paid, depending on the circumstances at the time. The business owner will pay tax on a portion of the premium that is returned, but it is smaller than the nearly 40 percent paid on your dividend. The $1 million of critical-illness insurance that was in place to protect your company for fifteen years in the event that you suffered a critical illness cost your company little or nothing, except in the interest you might have earned if you had put that same amount of money in another investment.

It's important to note here that this strategy is based on the laws governing Canadian insurance at the time of this writing. Those laws can change at any time. That said, even without the tax advantage, the premiums could be returned to your company after fifteen years. A bad scenario possible is that you'd have to pay a dividend on that amount at the time you draw it out of your company's operating account. In the meantime, your company was financially protected in the event you suffered a critical illness during that time.

PROTECTING KEY EMPLOYEES WHO AREN'T SHAREHOLDERS

Attracting and keeping key employees who aren't shareholders can be important to the overall success of your business. If one of these key employees suffered a critical illness, your company might suffer from the long-term loss of this person. Just like with you, the owner, your company is able to purchase critical-illness insurance that will pay your company in the event your employee is unable to work for an extended period of time.

You can also use this critical-illness insurance as a hook to help keep these important members of your team onboard using the split-dollar agreement. Let's say you carry critical-illness coverage on the employee. Again, the company is the beneficiary of that coverage because it is paying the premiums. But the company can have a rider on the policy that states that there can be a return of the premium after fifteen years. There can also be an agreement with the key employee that says that if the policy is unused for fifteen years, the premiums will be returned directly to the key employee. Knowing there's going to be a large cash payout after fifteen years of service to a company is a great incentive for keeping that employee over the long term. The key employee will only have a small taxable benefit for the part of the premium that pays for the reimbursement.

FUNDING BUY-SELL AGREEMENTS

Remember that unsigned partnership agreement I talked about in chapter 4? That's not the only ticking time bomb that may be hiding out in your partnership agreement.

During our initial assessment process, my partner and I work from the ground up to ensure that a company is built on a solid foundation. One of the important things we do is review any partnership agreements that are in place. One of the standard features of partnership agreements is a clause that requires the partners to have insurance in place in order to finance the buyback of corporate shares in the event that one of the partners dies or becomes disabled. It's a legal obligation . . . it's in the contract.

We've been in a number of situations in which we meet with partners and point out that they are legally obligated to buy out a partner who is disabled in twelve to twenty-four months, with eighteen months being the most common. The partners will tell us, "We don't want to pay for that," or "We don't need that." The problem isn't when nothing happens. The problem is when something happens, like when one partner gets into a serious automobile accident and is in a coma. After the eighteen months, the wife visits her lawyer, who contacts the surviving partner or partners and tells them to pay up under the terms of the contract.

If you're the party who is injured, it makes a whole lot of sense to have this clause in the partnership agreement. Let's go back to the three-partner scenario. Any one of the partners could be the injured party. Having the appropriate insurance in place to fund the repurchase agreement not only helps the injured partner's family but also ensures that the business can survive. Without this insurance coverage, the business will be legally obligated to come up with the cash to cover the repurchase of the insurance partner's shares in the company.

Not only does the company need to carry this type of insurance on the partners, but it's important that the coverage is reviewed from time to time and kept up to date. Here's why.

Let's say that when two people sign a fifty-fifty partnership agreement, their fledgling company is worth $1 million. So the amount of life insurance needed for the company to buy back shares from the beneficiaries in the event one partner dies is based on the value of the company at the time the partnership agreement was signed.

After five years of hard work, the company has grown in value to $10 million. But has the life-insurance protection grown accordingly? A partner dies suddenly, and the company is obligated per the partnership agreement to repurchase the interests of the now-deceased partner. Without life insurance, can the company afford to pay the family $5 million out-of-pocket? Or will the company have to be sold to meet its contractual obligation?

Oftentimes, we will recommend a twenty-year term insurance policy on each of the partners to cover the repurchase agreement in the event of death of one of the partners. During that twenty-year term, if the company isn't sold and continues to operate, the term insurance carried by the company can be converted to permanent insurance.

Another important consideration is that if you're the partner who dies, and the company immediately falls apart because you were the brains of the operation, you want your family to receive the value of its share of the company *before* you died, because the value of the company a moment after you die might be a lot less. So if your portion of the company is worth $2 million upon your death, you want to make sure there is $2 million of life insurance in place on you (and all the partners) of $2 million. The agreement states that you have to use the insurance in priority to pay the shares. In other words, the company can't take the life-insurance payout to buy new equipment instead of buying out your shares from your beneficiaries.

However, let's say you and your partners planned ahead and took out more life insurance than the company was worth, because you were anticipating future growth. Instead of $2 million for each partner, the company took out $5 million of life-insurance coverage on each. Provided that the partnership agreement specifically states that the value of the company is calculated on the amount of the life insurance that comes in, that means that if there's $5 million in life-insurance coverage on a partner, that partner's beneficiaries will receive the entire $5 million, even if that partner's shares aren't worth $5 million. On the other hand, it's important to note that in this case, if the partner's shares are valued at $5.5 million at the time of death, the company will use the $5 million from the life-insurance payout and still have to come up with the additional $500,000.

As you can see, it's important to the long-term health of your company that your company's insurance needs are reviewed annually to make sure they are in line with the actual value of the business. It's always better to have a little more insurance than needed than a little less. I've never heard from a beneficiary that the shareholder left him or her too much money in life insurance.

It is also common that partnership agreements provide that if a partner is disabled for twelve to twenty-four months, depending on the terms of the agreement, the one partner is obligated to buy back the shares of the disabled partner. Disability insurance carried on the partners will help provide financially for the health and longevity of the company.

CHAPTER 8

CROSSING THE FINISH LINE

STRATEGIES FOR RETIREMENT PLANNING

As you build your business, it's important to start building a retirement strategy as soon as possible. Because the markets are volatile, putting at least a portion of your retirement money into a stable product that is not subject to the major fluctuations of the markets is vital to your future.

For example, let's say you own a business that sells eggs. You are making a lot of money with your egg business and it has continued to grow, year after year. Then one day there is a report that eggs are a major cause of some terrible disease. What's going to happen to your egg business, and what about your plans for retirement? You probably don't really own an egg business, but I'm sure you understand my point. Putting away a certain amount of your income every year will help you retire in comfort, even if you face a few tough years along the way.

We recommend that you put some, if not all, of your personal retirement money into segregated funds, many of which you purchase through insurance companies. If the worst happens and your company goes into bankruptcy, the funds in segregated funds cannot be seized. Let's say your company is sued for malpractice or for back taxes the government has determined you owe. That lawsuit can take your company down, but what the lawyers and the government won't have access to is the money you have in segregated funds.

RRSPv AND TFSA

In Section One of this book, I explained the importance of funding a portion of your retirement through two types of tax-sheltered savings accounts. In 1957, Canada introduced the Registered Retirement Savings Plan to help promote savings for retirement. These accounts, which hold savings and investment assets, have various tax advantages compared to unsheltered accounts. Approved assets that can be held in RRSPs include bonds, income trusts, corporate shares, savings accounts, mutual funds, labor-sponsored funds, and guaranteed-investment certificates.

Contributions made to an RRSP are tax-deductible, and taxes are deferred until the money is withdrawn. At retirement, your marginal tax rate could be lower.

For example, let's say that today your tax rate is 50 percent. For every $100 you invest in your RRSP up to your contribution limit, you will save $50 in taxes. Additionally, growth of the investments in your RRSP is tax sheltered and therefore exempt from any capital-gains taxes or income taxes. While RRSPs are made up of mutual funds, they are unseizable in bankruptcy.

In 2009, Canada started the Tax-Free Savings Account program as a way for adults to set aside money tax-free throughout their lifetimes. Contributions to a TFSA are not deductible for income-tax purposes, but any amount contributed, as well as any income earned in this type of account, is generally tax-free, even when it is withdrawn. TFSAs can provide a secondary way for you to save for retirement.

Good retirement planning begins with maximizing your tax-sheltered RRSPs and TFSAs. Because you'll be able to save using these options for a long time, a large amount of money will accumulate for use when you're no longer working.

As a successful business owner, chances are you've been saving for retirement for a while. But as you're learning, there are other tax-efficient ways to build an even larger retirement nest egg using insurance products. One potential way is through your unused critical-illness policy.

STRATEGY FOR USING CRITICAL-ILLNESS INSURANCE TO FUND RETIREMENT

Let's say you paid $5,000 per year for a million-dollar critical-illness protection, and you did that for twenty years. That means that at the end of that twenty years, you've paid $100,000 for a critical-illness policy that you haven't needed. Now that you're retiring, you decide that because you are financially independent, you don't need it anymore. If you get sick, you can take care of the expenses on your own. At that point, you can cancel the policy and be reimbursed for the entire $100,000 you spent. That means you purchased that $1 million of protection for whatever you could have earned in interest if you had invested that $100,000 elsewhere.

STRATEGY FOR USING LIFE INSURANCE TO FUND RETIREMENT

When business owners don't need as much life insurance as they once did because they are retired, their kids are independent, and they don't have a mortgage payment every month, they can use life insurance as an income for retirement. This works much like using an unused critical-illness policy purchased by your company.

Here's an example: When you are forty years old, your company takes out a participating life-insurance policy with a face value (or death benefit) of $1 million. The annual premium on that policy is $5,000, which is paid by the company for twenty years. A portion of the premium is invested and can earn dividends that are added to your policy's cash value. Once you reach age sixty-five, that policy will likely have a cash value of about $1.4 million—tax-free until it's taken out.

At age sixty-five, you've decided to retire. You've left a lot of money in your corporation, but now you want a portion of the cash value of your life-insurance policy to help fund your retirement. In order to get the money out of the corporate coffers into your own pocket, you will have to declare a dividend and pay about 40 percent taxes on the amount you take. But is there a way to have access to that money without paying those high taxes on it? Now here's where this strategy gets interesting.

The business owner can go to a bank and take out a line of credit using the $1.4 million cash value of the life-insurance policy as collateral. Because the cash values in the participating life-insurance policy are crystalized every year, that means the cash value can't go down. It's guaranteed, so the bank will agree to open a personal line of credit for you for about 90 percent of the cash value, or $1.26 million. You'll have access to that entire amount tax-free because it's a debt. Most of the time, you won't even have to pay the monthly interest to the bank. When you die, the death benefit will go to your company because it's the owner of the life-insurance policy. Once the money is placed in your company's capital-dividend account, your beneficiaries will have access to that money at a low tax rate. They will repay the bank for the principal and interest it's owed on the line of credit . . . all that money you used tax-free while you were still alive without having to declare a dividend. You will also pay taxes on the difference between what you were charged with the line of credit secured by collateral, and the rate you would have paid if you had gotten the line of credit without guarantees on your own. For example, that could be the difference between the 3 percent interest on a line of credit guaranteed by a life-insurance policy, and a 6 percent personal line of credit with no guarantees. That amounts to a very low tax rate compared to what you would have paid if you'd taken a dividend from your company.

CHAPTER 9

PASSING THE BATON

STRATEGIES FOR BUSINESS SUCCESSION

REAL-LIFE SCENARIO

My business partner and I were completing a business assessment of a large company here in Montreal. The owner, who was nearly seventy years of age, had worked hard his entire life and had his eye on retiring soon so that he could enjoy life while he was still healthy. The man employed his oldest son as the company's general manager and expected that he would take over as president when the owner retired, and his daughter worked in the business as a marketing assistant. The man also had another son, who worked for another company as an auto mechanic. This son had never been involved with his father's company. Upon review of the business owner's will and trust, we discovered that he wanted to divide his company equally between his three children. "I want to treat my children the same, so the company must be divided equally between them," the business owner insisted.

Despite the business owner's good intentions, dividing the company between his three children is actually anything but equal. In this type of circumstance, which we see often, we typically ask the business owner how the children working in the business will feel about working the remaining years of their careers to give a third of their corporate profits to the one child who is not involved with the company. We then point out that there are other ways to make the business succession equal without splitting the company three ways.

Because the business was worth $5 million, the business owner took out a life-insurance policy (paid by the company) for $10 million. Upon his death, 100 percent of the business shares would go to the son who was already involved in running the company, thus ensuring the business would continue operating. The $10 million in life insurance would be split between the owner's daughter and other son.

There's a big problem brewing in Canada. A look down the road ten years into the future reveals that there are few young people interested in taking over existing businesses, even those built by one of their parents. Because of that, there are a large number of business owners who don't have a succession plan in place for their business.

For a business owner who is lucky enough to have a natural successor like a son or daughter who wants to take over, it is important to understand and appreciate that the child will be investing a major portion of his or her life into the company. As the prior real-life scenario illustrates, dividing the company equally between siblings may not be the best option for the succession of the company or for the one child who will continue what you started. Therefore, the business owner must consider carefully whether equal division of a company among children is always the best strategy. Is this one child expected to give up a portion of the profits to the other siblings for the rest of his or her life? We see all too often how such arrangements can destroy not only the company, but also the family. So it's extremely important to the continuation of the business to understand all your options and how they can be funded. In the end, life insurance may be the most effective means to achieve equality among your children.

It's also important to note that you need to have the right insurance coverage in place to avoid the successor having to sell a portion of the business to pay the taxes upon your death.

While you're still healthy, it's a good idea to sit down with your entire family to discuss the future of your company. The last thing you want is for the family to split over a decision you made in a vacuum.

Let's take another look at exactly how this works.

BUSINESS SUCCESSION STRATEGY

Part of the extensive assessment we conduct involves making sure that the business owner's will and trust are in order. These important documents can play an important role in the continuation of the business upon the death of its owner.

Here's the scenario we see all too often.

The owner has worked for thirty years to build a successful business. Because he loves his two children, his will states that the shares of his business will be split equally between his children upon his death. That's only fair, right?

But let's say that his daughter has worked side by side with him in the business for the last fifteen years. She loves the family business, knows the ins and outs of its workings, has built relationships with the employees and clients, and has been the person the business owner has come to rely on to get the job done in all situations.

On the other hand, his son studied to become a veterinarian and is currently working as a professional in another part of the province. Over the years, the son has shown no interest in the family business, is completely focused on his new profession, and has plans to open his own veterinary clinic sometime in the future.

When the daughter takes over running the business upon the death of her father, she can expect to work the remaining years of her career with 50 percent of every cent of profit she makes going to her brother, who has never been involved with the business. That's on top of the brother's own substantial income he's earning as a veterinarian.

For the business owner who wanted the division of his life work to be equitable between his children, is this really fair? The daughter working for the rest of her career to give half of what she earns to her brother would probably say no.

Rather than letting the two children fight it out once he's dead, the business owner needs to understand that there may be a better way to handle the business succession. We often suggest that in situations like this, 100 percent of the business shares should go to the child who is actively involved with the business, which also helps ensure the succession of the business. Then we work to make sure that the other child receives an amount of money or assets that is equal to the value of the business at the time of the business owner's death.

For example, let's say the business is worth $5 million upon the death of the owner. The daughter will receive 100 percent of the shares of the business, while the son will receive $5 million worth of cash or other assets. Maybe the owner has a cottage or other assets that can go to the son. We work with the business owner to make sure that it is an equitable division that works for both children.

If the owner has most of his assets tied up in the company, which is typical for many successful business owners, then we make sure there is enough life insurance in place so that the son will get his inheritance in a cash payout from that policy.

One of the business owners we worked with told me, "Power can't be shared in a family business." That reinforced what I've learned through the years—that it's important to choose one of the children to be in charge upon the death of the owner, while making sure the other child or children are compensated in ways other than in shares of the business.

It's always a good idea for the business owner to sit down with his children to discuss his plans before changing his will or trust. Usually, the family can come to a mutual understanding, which helps prevent fighting and long-term animosities among siblings later on. In the case of the daughter and son I described above, both were ecstatic with the new plan.

BUSINESS SUCCESSION STRATEGY WHEN THERE'S NO NATURAL SUCCESSOR

As I've pointed out before, it's important for business owners to have an exit strategy. Depending on what area of business you are in, some businesses have almost no value or are only worth the value of the in-store inventory if you don't have someone on the inside positioned to buy out the business when you retire. The reality is, your competitors will let the business die rather than buy you out because they know they will get the customers anyway. If you're lucky, a competitor will buy you out at a low price.

In order to get the value of your business at retirement, you have to think ahead about a successor (provided you don't already have a natural successor such as a son, daughter, brother, niece, etc.). Here's why it's so important to plan ahead: when you sell shares of your business in Canada, you are allowed up to an $800,000 tax exception on capital gains. That's equivalent to earning $1.6 million in taxable income. So selling your business stock to a willing buyer can put a large sum of money into your pocket tax-free, adding greatly to your retirement lifestyle.

Between five and ten years prior to when you plan to retire, bring a young entrepreneur into your business with the goal of grooming him or her to buy out the business when you retire. Teach that person how the business works and introduce him or her to your customers. Then, when you decide to retire, you can sell your business shares to that person, a willing successor who is eager to carry on the work you started.

I can't stress enough just how important this is for you to think about. So often, successful business owners are so busy working their businesses that they wait until a year or two before retirement to bring in someone to take over. You never know—maybe the first person you bring in isn't the right one, so you may have to look for someone else, so give yourself enough time to find the perfect replacement.

Grooming the right person to buy out your business shares upon your retirement not only allows you to sell the business you've built over the years for what it's worth, but it also allows you to train your successor as a person your customers know will fill your shoes. Your customers will already know your successor because he or she has been around for a while, and they will continue to do business with the company after you're gone. You can even make a deal with your buyer to stay on full or part time after you sell to help ensure a smooth transition. That's what I call sound financial planning.

Upon retirement, you can close your business or sell your business shares at a ridiculous price, leaving tax-free dollars on the table. Or you can plan early for your succession upon your retirement to get the maximum amount of benefit for the years of hard work you've put into growing a successful business.

STRATEGY FOR COVERING CAPITAL-GAINS TAXES OWED ON REAL ESTATE

I talked about this strategy in chapter 5, but I think it's important to review in the context of a business succession that involves a large amount of real estate. We have a case right now with a seventy-eight-year-old real estate investor who is worth about $15 million. His properties are a mix of residential and commercial, which he rents out to earn an income. Comparing the value of the property now with what he paid for it reveals that there's a capital gain of about $10 million, which is taxed at 25 percent. When he dies, it's a fact that he will have to pay $2.5 million in capital-gains taxes. That's a $2.5 million tax for his succession, which is his wife and children.

The best option would have been to make sure that there is $2.5 million to pay the tax, either in one bank account or one other investment. In this case, there isn't. Very often, real estate investors don't have a lot of cash flow, because as soon as they get a lump sum of money, they buy another property. They don't want that kind of money sleeping in a bank account or other investment, because they know that buying real estate is a great investment.

My client told me that his successors would have to take a mortgage on some of the properties to pay the $2.5 million in taxes. But I know from experience that real estate investors tend to also use any available equity in a property to buy another property. So, often, the beneficiaries can't even get a mortgage.

I also pointed out that even if they can get a mortgage to pay the $2.5 million in capital-gains taxes, the interest they will pay on this mortgage loan will not be tax-deductible, because it's not being used to make more money and is therefore not a business expense. I told him that the best way to cover the $2.5 million would be through life insurance, which would probably cost him $350,000 per year because of his age. He was quick to point out that $350,000 per year is a lot of money, but when I told him he could get the life insurance without too much effect on his cash flow, he was all ears.

"But what's the catch?" he asked. I explained that my company has access to banks that are willing to open lines of credit for our clients that can be used to help them pay the premium on a participating ("par") life-insurance policy. Initially, the bank will agree to guarantee the loan up to 90 percent of the cash value of the life-insurance product and the real estate owned by the investor. So the bank pays the $350,000 per year for the par life insurance, which grows at an interest rate that is around prime. Our strategy is to make sure that at any given moment, there's enough life insurance to pay the $2.5 million in taxes plus the value of the line of credit. In this example, based on his life expectancy of ten years, we make sure that he will have $6 million, which includes $2.5 million for his successors to pay his capital-gains taxes and to repay the bank for the line of credit used to pay his annual premiums plus interest. Everyone's happy.

Upon the investor's death, his family can continue operating the business. They will avoid having to sell off a portion of the property to pay the tax bill. They will also avoid another major problem I've seen frequently.

Let's say the real estate investor purchased a property ten years ago for $300,000. Today it's worth $1 million, but as the property's value increased, the investor used the equity to purchase another property. The mortgage on it is now $800,000. When his successors sell it off for $1 million, they will receive $200,000. But remember, they will owe capital-gains taxes on $700,000, or $175,000 (today's value of $1 million – the original price of $300,000 × the 25 percent tax rate). That leaves them only $25,000 to use towards the $2.5 million in taxes still owed. Now not only is the $1 million property gone but so is the income the business earned by renting it out.

The worst-case scenario for the successors is that they are pressed to get the capital-gains taxes paid off on the properties left to them by the real estate investor within the short period allowed by the government. But what happens if the market is down? The government has determined that based on the fair market value, the building is worth $1 million. But the successors can only get $800,000 for it, all of which goes directly to the bank to pay off the mortgage. They've received no money to pay on the $2.5 million, and now they owe an additional amount of taxes on the property. As a real estate investor, it's easy to see that you might have a succession that ends up losing it all in trying to pay the taxes. The best solution is to have a life-insurance policy in place that will cover the capital-gains taxes. Life insurance is perfect for solving these types of problems. It can be put in place to cover any taxes that might be owed upon the death of a business owner.

CHAPTER 10

ANCILLARY TRAINING

STRATEGIES FOR PLANNED GIVING

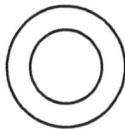

O ver the course of my career as a financial security advisor, it has been my pleasure to work with successful business owners who share my values. My clients tend to be people just like me who love their families and not only desire to leave the next generation better off but are willing to do whatever it takes to make that happen.

It just so happens that these successful business owners are usually the very same people who give back to the communities in which they live. Volunteering your time and money is personally rewarding and a way to ensure brighter futures for all the members of our towns and cities, our province, and our country.

Giving to your favorite foundation can begin with a monthly contribution of both your time and your money. In fact, we believe in giving back so much that we encourage all of our clients to incorporate a planned giving strategy right into their annual budgets.

Of course, I have my favorite charities to which I passionately give my time and money. I am always happy to make suggestions if you are looking for a worthy cause to support.

For the last few years, I've been involved with the Foundation of Stars, which supports research on childhood diseases. I recently began working with the Heart and Stroke Foundation of Québec by getting involved in a committee. The vision of this foundation is to promote healthy lives free of heart disease and stroke across the province. As research organizations, both the Foundation of Stars and the Heart and Stroke Foundation of Québec can potentially have an impact that is far reaching. Of course, donating money is important, but my staff and I love getting involved with organizing and attending events that benefit these important foundations.

Right before Christmas every year, I reach out to three to five underprivileged families with serious money issues. Most often, it's a single-parent family that just needs a hand up. I take the parent grocery shopping to fill their cupboards ahead of the holidays, and I make sure the family gets the treats they can't normally afford during the year. This is giving just for the sake of giving—I expect nothing in return. It's a very gratifying aspect of my life.

As a successful business owner who has put all the right financial strategies into place, you will be transferring a large amount of wealth to your spouse and your children. But what about your favorite charities and foundations?

If you have one or more charitable foundations that are close to your heart, you can name them as beneficiary to a portion of your life insurance. Doing this serves two important purposes. A large gift to a hospital or foundation can have a major impact on the future of many lives. But also, there are tax advantages to giving a large charitable contribution from your life insurance. A large contribution to your favorite foundation will serve as a tax deduction on your final tax return.

Because of the many tax strategies we help put into place for our clients, our hope is that the companies we serve will, in turn, serve their community by donating a small portion of their profits. Giving is so easy to build right into a corporate budget, and there are a number of tax benefits for sharing a corporation's wealth.

WINNING THE RACE

Whether you are a self-employed professional just starting out or a seasoned business owner with a successful company, there are a number of financial strategies that can help you protect and build your wealth.

Through our years of experience, we know that self-employed professionals who are just starting out often begin their careers with little or no understanding of how to plan for their financial futures. We can help them get on the right path early on so that they can focus on their careers.

My special area of focus is helping successful business owners. Through the years, my company has developed a nontraditional approach to problem solving, as well as wealth protection and growth. I use in-depth knowledge of specific financial products to help business owners reap the greatest tax advantages that are legally available. It's not that your other financial advisors failed to tell you about these strategies; it's more likely that they simply didn't know about them. Whatever your destination, we'll be there to recommend a route to get you there.

www.ingramcontent.com/pod-product-compliance
Lightning Source LLC
Chambersburg PA
CBHW050509210326
41521CB00011B/2387

* 9 7 8 1 5 9 9 3 2 7 1 2 9 *